A SHERLOCK HOLMES DEVOTIONAL

A SHERLOCK HOLMES DEVOTIONAL

UNCOVERING THE MYSTERIES OF GOD

TRISHA WHITE PRIEBE

SHILOH RUN PRESS
An Imprint of Barbour Publishing, Inc.

© 2015 by Trisha White Priebe.

Print ISBN 978-1- 63058-912-7

eBook Editions:
Adobe Digital Edition (.epub) 978-1-63409-543-3
Kindle and MobiPocket Edition (.prc) 978-1-63409-544-0

All rights reserved. No part of this publication may be reproduced or transmitted for commercial purposes, except for brief quotations in printed reviews, without written permission of the publisher.

Churches and other noncommercial interests may reproduce portions of this book without the express written permission of Barbour Publishing, provided that the text does not exceed 500 words or 5 percent of the entire book, whichever is less, and that the text is not material quoted from another publisher. When reproducing text from this book, include the following credit line: "From *A Sherlock Holmes Devotional: Uncovering the Mysteries of God*, published by Barbour Publishing, Inc. Used by permission."

Scripture quotations marked KJV are taken from the King James Version of the Bible.

Scripture quotations marked NKJV are taken from the New King James Version®. Copyright © 1982 by Thomas Nelson, Inc. Used by permission. All rights reserved.

Scripture quotations marked NIV are taken from the HOLY BIBLE, NEW INTERNATIONAL VERSION®. NIV®. Copyright © 1973, 1978, 1984, 2011 by Biblica, Inc.™ Used by permission. All rights reserved worldwide.

Scripture quotations marked ESV are from The Holy Bible, English Standard Version®, copyright © 2001 by Crossway Bibles, a publishing ministry of Good News Publishers. Used by permission. All rights reserved.

Scripture quotations marked NLT are taken from the *Holy Bible,* New Living Translation copyright© 1996, 2004, 2007 by Tyndale House Foundation. Used by permission of Tyndale House Publishers, Inc. Carol Stream, Illinois 60188. All rights reserved.

Scripture quotations marked NASB are taken from the New American Standard Bible®, © 1960, 1962, 1963, 1968, 1971, 1972, 1973, 1975, 1977, 1995 by The Lockman Foundation. Used by permission.

Cover design: Kirk DouPonce, DogEared Design

Published by Shiloh Run Press, an imprint of Barbour Publishing, Inc., P.O. Box 719, Uhrichsville, Ohio 44683, www.shilohrunpress.com

Our mission is to publish and distribute inspirational products offering exceptional value and biblical encouragement to the masses.

Member of the
Evangelical Christian
Publishers Association

Printed in the United States of America.

DEDICATION

To Randy and Faith White

My mom, the English teacher, spent her summer breaks reading to my brother and me from paperback classics and crimson hardcovers with her golden voice and vibrant expression. And I can hear my dad, the high school chemistry teacher, hunched over his lab table— test tubes in hand and Bunsen burner aglow—shouting, "I've found it!" when an experiment succeeded. Loving Sherlock Holmes was written in my DNA.

CONTENTS

INTRODUCTION

To read and love Sherlock Holmes is to forget that he is a work of fiction.

Millions of people spanning three centuries have been impressed and inspired by this towering genius with the piercing stare and unyielding determination who could solve the most formidable of crimes in the time it took the average person to compose a simple grocery list.

So real is this detective that people often talk about him as if he were a human being and not the creation of Arthur Conan Doyle's brilliant imagination. Entire literary societies argue with conviction that no obituary was ever printed in London's *The Times*, meaning Holmes wasn't only real, but he also never actually died.

Meaning, in the minds of some, he could still be alive and well somewhere.

Sound crazy to argue over the life and death of a fictional character? Maybe. But crazier things have happened. As one of the three most easily recognizable characters in the world (the other two being Santa Claus and Mickey Mouse), Sherlock Holmes is a household name, responsible for uniting readers in all stages of life and igniting conversations fueled by observation, passion, and intelligence.

Whether each reader was first introduced to *The Adventures of Sherlock Holmes* by a parent, a teacher, or a personal voyage into the stories by a weak lamplight at bedtime, the truth remains: A century after stepping onto the page and into the hearts of readers, Sherlock Holmes is, indeed, alive and well. More people read and admire this fictional character today than ever before.

The reason is simple.

Through Arthur Conan Doyle's stories, collectively called *the canon*, Holmes continues to leave endless clues that teach us timeless truths about ourselves. And if we take the time to apply careful deduction—as Holmes would have done—we can even learn an object lesson or two about the enduring mysteries of God.

So whether this is your first study of Sherlock Holmes or whether, like me, you are a closet Sherlockian at heart, it is my sincerest hope that what you find in the following pages only deepens your understanding of the Master and the mastermind.

1.

THE ART OF LISTENING

*"There is no part of the body which
varies so much as the human ear."*
THE ADVENTURE OF THE CARDBOARD BOX

Sherlock Holmes. The world's first consulting detective whose services are equal parts eccentric and extraordinary.

For more than one hundred years, writers have created variations and spin-offs of the unconventional detective—crafting characters who are wholly unsympathetic and utterly brilliant. Novelists and scriptwriters alike in the twenty-first century often attribute the inspiration behind their curmudgeon characters to the detective in the deerstalker cap.

Sherlock Holmes is truly *the man, the myth, the legend.*

Literature is littered with famous detectives—G. K. Chesterton's Father Brown, Edgar Allan Poe's Dupin, Agatha Christie's Miss Marple, and Carolyn Keene's Nancy Drew—to name a few, but none are as well known or fiercely loved as Sherlock Holmes. He is timeless in his fan base and enduring in his readership. Students of the great detective cherish their well-worn copies of Sir Arthur Conan Doyle's stories with as much loyalty today as they did in 1887 when Sherlock Holmes first dashed onto the published page.

So what makes Sherlock Holmes great? Simply put, he had abnormally sharp senses. He could hear and see things missed by the ordinary man. In fact, in one of Doyle's short stories, "The Adventure of the Three Gables," it is even implied that the mastermind could smell things missed by everyone else—identifying a stranger on his doorstep as coming from the odorous Old Nichol, an area of East London where the worst criminals did their horrific deeds.

This uncanny attention to detail enables Sherlock to solve the most intimidating crimes without so much as a hint of anxiety. Fans of Sherlock Holmes read the mysteries—not to see *if*, but to marvel *how* he will solve them.

"The Adventure of the Cardboard Box" is another of the fifty-six original short stories featuring Sherlock Holmes. The story begins, so Doyle writes, on "a blazing hot day in August. Baker Street was like an oven, and the glare of the sunlight upon the yellow brickwork of the house across the road was painful to the eye."[1] Enter Miss Susan Cushing, a woman with a placid face and large, gentle eyes. She had received a package in the mail containing two severed human ears. Miss Cushing is understandably horrified, but the police are convinced it was nothing more than a practical joke, played on Miss Cushing by medical students with too much time on their hands and an extra cadaver in their possession. Sherlock Holmes does not agree with the police and quickly begins to make his case that the ears were actually the evidence of a grizzly crime.

Sherlock Holmes will be right, of course. Sherlock Holmes is always right.

As the story unfolds, Holmes makes the famous statement: "There is no part of the body which varies so much as the human ear."[2] And while in the story he was speaking specifically about the *organ* that detects sound, the same could be said about the *act* of listening.

One of the most passionately debated topics within Christianity today involves hearing the voice of God. Few Christians would deny that God speaks to His children, but how, where, when, and why are matters of endless debate.

Where should I go to college? Whom should I marry? What career should I pursue? Where should I live?

These questions—and others like them—are just the tip of the iceberg as it pertains to knowing and doing God's will. Like Samuel in the Old Testament, we wish to say, "Speak, LORD, for Your servant hears" (1 Samuel 3:9 ESV), yet we aren't entirely sure what we should listen for in response. We know our obligation is to hear and heed, but how?

The answer lies in the indisputable, indestructible, all-sufficient Word of God. Hebrews 4:12 tells us that the Bible is alive and active. The opposite of an outdated volume left to gather dust on a shelf, the Bible works like a surgeon, carefully cutting away the dead parts of our hearts and breathing life into our weary souls. Better still, the Bible contains the answer to every question we will ever ask that pertains to our obedience to God. Our heavenly Father does not act as a type of Easter Bunny, hiding His will in tiny colored eggs and waiting for us to discover them. He wants us to know His will for our lives.

We need no extra system. God has given us everything we need for life and godliness.

The truth is that God is and always has been more devoted to His will than we will ever be, so that if we go to Him in prayer with a humble heart and the desire to obey, He will always meet us with grace and guidance in a voice that is unmistakably His.

Prayer and Bible reading are the clearest means we have to hear the voice of God.

"Speak, for your servant hears."
1 SAMUEL 3:10 ESV

2.

DEATH OF A DETECTIVE

"There is nothing like firsthand evidence."
A Study in Scarlet

Sherlock Holmes made his first appearance in the novel *A Study in Scarlet* when Dr. Watson, looking for a roommate, arrived at the chemical lab in the hospital where Holmes was working.

The scene was set. Sherlock Holmes sat in:

A lofty chamber, lined and littered with countless bottles. Broad, low tables were scattered about, which bristled with retorts, test tubes, and little Bunsen lamps, with their blue flickering flames.[1]

Holmes sat alone, hunched over his table, absorbed in his work. When he eventually realized someone had come to visit, he jumped up, test tube in hand, and ran around the room yelling, "I've found it! I've found it!"[2]

Can you imagine? This little charade probably should have scared Dr. Watson from ever wanting to live with the great detective. Instead, it spawned the most famous crime-solving duo in history. Dr. Watson did, of course, become

Holmes' roommate and lifelong friend.

From that first story, *A Study in Scarlet*, published in 1887, readers chose to believe Sherlock Holmes was a real person and not the cleverly crafted character from Sir Arthur Conan Doyle's imagination. Ask any Sherlock Holmes devotee if the detective is merely a work of fiction, and then prepare yourself for an adamant response: "Absolutely not!"

An estimate of Holmes' age, based on the birth year 1854, taken from "His Last Bow," means he would now be 161 years old, and still some devotees claim the detective is alive and well.

When Doyle eventually decided he was tired of writing about the detective—believing Sherlock Holmes was preventing him from pursuing other literary goals—Doyle decided to kill off his creation. Easy enough.

Readers couldn't demand more stories if the lead character was dead.

Right?

The public was so outraged by the death of their beloved detective that they wore black armbands in a show of solidarity and mourning. Thousands of people canceled their subscriptions to *The Strand Magazine*, where Doyle's short stories were published, and letters from devastated readers poured in from around the world.

Fans of Sherlock Holmes took—and still take—the detective seriously.

It was in the fourth chapter of that first story where it all began, *A Study in Scarlet*, that Holmes uttered the famous line, "There is nothing like firsthand evidence."[3]

He was right, of course.

The Bible is full of exhortations to know God personally. We have the ability—and even the mandate—to gather firsthand evidence about our heavenly Father. Two great tools in our toolbox for gathering these facts are prayer and Bible reading.

Prayer was designed for pursuit of relationship with Him. One of the great gifts Christ gave us when He laid down His life was the ability to bypass a priest in order to gain personal access to God. No longer are we at the mercy of another human being to represent us before the Almighty. With a mere thought or whisper, we are transported into the throne room of God.

Scripture reading, too, was designed for us to learn more about our Savior. In centuries past, people were too poor or too illiterate to read the Bible for themselves. In medieval times, the Catholic Church opposed Bible reading by the common man. Throughout the ages various people have maintained a mind-set that scripture reading was intended for pastors or scholars.

These people are partially correct.

Bible reading is for pastors and scholars *and everyone else*. Diligence, not intelligence, is the primary key to unlocking the mysteries of the Bible.

Though it is good for us to sit under the careful instruction of pastors or teachers who love God, nothing has the power to change us like a firsthand relationship with our heavenly Father. We must study the scriptures for ourselves, tracing God's hand in the workings of history and piecing together the clues of His character. If it was important for Jesus to withdraw from the crowds in order to spend time alone with His Father (see Matthew 26:36), certainly it is no less essential for us to do the same.

We should ask ourselves the following three questions whenever we approach a passage in the Bible: *What can I discover about God? What can I learn about the world? What can I apply to my life?*

We ought to devote ourselves to daily, personal worship. We should also participate in the privilege of corporate worship at church with brothers and sisters in Christ, compelling those with whom we worship to admire God the way we do.

C. S. Lewis, who was a contemporary of Conan Doyle, reflected on the Psalms, writing:

Just as men spontaneously praise whatever they value,
so they spontaneously urge us to join them in praising it:
"Isn't she lovely? Wasn't it glorious? Don't you think that
magnificent?" The Psalmists in telling everyone to praise

God are doing what all men do when they speak of what they care about.[4]

Little is more powerful than a Christian whose life is invested in the pursuit of God.

> *Taste and see that the LORD is good.*
> *Oh, the joys of those who take refuge in him!*
> PSALM 34:8 NLT

3.

MAN BEHIND THE MASK

"You see, but you do not observe.
The distinction is clear."
A SCANDAL IN BOHEMIA

Sherlock Holmes is a master of disguise.

Throughout the four novels and fifty-six short stories in which he is featured, Sherlock often conceals his identity in order to get a closer look at the criminal or to gain better access to critical evidence. His creative disguises include an Italian priest, an elderly scholar, an old woman, an asthmatic old master mariner, and an Irish-American spy.

In "A Scandal in Bohemia," Sherlock Holmes was so convincing when he masqueraded as a drunk groom that even his faithful sidekick, Dr. Watson, became confused, saying:

It was close upon four before the door opened, and a
drunken-looking groom, ill-kempt and side-whiskered,
with an inflamed face and disreputable clothes, walked
into the room. Accustomed as I was to my friend's
amazing powers in the use of disguises, I had to look
three times before I was certain that it was indeed he.[1]

Unfortunately, despite Holmes' amazing powers in the use of disguises, one person outsmarted Holmes in this same story. A woman named Irene Adler was also a master of disguise, and while dressed like a young boy, she slipped out from under Holmes' nose and got away with the much-sought-after photograph that Holmes needed to close his case.

Given Holmes' general opinion of women, it is ironic that Irene Adler outsmarted him. In the only story in which Holmes was ever defeated, Holmes was beaten by a woman's wit. The final lines of "A Scandal in Bohemia" read: "And when he speaks of Irene Adler, or when he refers to her photograph, it is always under the honourable title of *the woman*."[2]

"A Scandal in Bohemia" is a short story about two clever people who sought to outsmart each other by using disguises. Either person could have won the challenge simply by seeing what was in front of his or her eyes. The truth was there all along.

So it is with God's Word.

Sometimes when we hit the speed bumps of life, we are tempted to read our Bibles and think—if not actually say—"Nothing in this Book was written to me! None of it applies to my specific situation." A quick search of your Bible's index will not find verses under the headings "unemployment," "stress," or "cancer," it's true. God's Word is silent about how, specifically, to navigate the teenage years in a public school or how to vote at the next election.

But God's Word remains wholly relevant to the events of our lives.

A closer look at the Bible will reveal God's desire for how we handle all of the issues we face. More surprising still, the Bible addresses every believer in every country at every age in every situation. Despite vast differences in time and place, God's Word, inspired thousands of years ago, was written for our edification.

In 1 Corinthians 10, Paul is speaking to first-century believers when he writes about the Israelites who grumbled and complained. Paul then makes a leap of many miles and many more years and says to his audience, "Now these things happened to them as an example, but they were written down for our instruction" (1 Corinthians 10:11 ESV).

If Paul believed it was appropriate to use a biblical example from a previous millennium to speak to the needs of his current audience, surely we can choose to do the same. The key is a willingness to spend the time and effort to study the scriptures and apply them appropriately.

To be certain, Bible reading is hard work. Why else do so many believers who love God struggle with consistency of spending time in the Word? If it were easy, everyone would do it.

Wisdom requires that we see God's Word—true and timeless—and apply it to our lives. So that we can walk with

Adam and Eve, travel with the Israelites, mourn with King David, and sit with Paul, all while applying the lessons each has to teach us to our situations. "All Scripture is breathed out by God and profitable for teaching, for reproof, for correction, and for training in righteousness" (2 Timothy 3:16 ESV).

If God were not certain that the men and women in the Bible had something of significance to offer to our lives, He would not have included them in a Book that has stood the test of time.

Reading the Bible is never less strenuous than the process of reading, but it is always more valuable than simply reading for reading's sake. If we come to the pages of scripture and do not see in them the guidance to navigate everyday life, we should say as Holmes did: "You see, but you do not observe. The distinction is clear."[3]

We must ask God to remove the blinders from our eyes so that we can see clearly the truths He has laid out for us. There is perhaps no shorter track to spiritual destruction than not reading and applying the Word of God in the way that He intended.

Open my eyes that I may see
wonderful things in your law.
PSALM 119:18 NIV

4.

AN UNLIKELY FRIENDSHIP

*"If you will treat me as a friend and trust me,
you may find that I will justify your trust."*
THE ADVENTURE OF ABBEY GRANGE

Sherlock Holmes is the definition of *peculiar*, no question about it.

From our first glimpse of this unconventional character, we see that he is poor enough to need a roommate, yet demanding enough to be without one. He is usually right, yet generally untactful. He is incredibly smart, yet often unwise. A collection of Sherlock Holmes' adventures reveals that he is brusque, stubborn, messy, and arrogant.

At first glance, Sherlock Holmes' personality leaves little by way of redemption.

So what could readers possibly have seen in Holmes to warrant fifty-six short stories and four novels? Furthermore, what is it about this prickly detective that has drawn readers to him like moths to a flame for more than a century?

Many classic characters with unsavory qualities have appeared on the published page and been left to gather dust in the library (Grendel's mother, anyone?). No one has offered to write a spin-off series honoring the White Witch from

Lewis's *The Lion, The Witch, and the Wardrobe*. No fan clubs have been constructed to study Shere Khan, the evil tiger who appears in Rudyard Kipling's *Jungle Book*, in greater detail.

And yet, entire societies devote their time and energy to Sherlock Holmes.

One indispensible characteristic that sets Sherlock apart from other heroes and antiheroes is his allegiance to his roommate and friend, Dr. Watson. Despite Sherlock's antisocial tendencies (an understatement if we're being honest), it becomes clear fairly quickly in each story that he is fiercely loyal to his friend.

In "The Adventure of Abbey Grange," Sherlock Holmes is speaking to Lady Brackenstall—the longsuffering wife of an abusive man who has been murdered—and a conversation ensues that is perhaps more personally revealing than Holmes intended it to be.

> *"I hope," said the lady, "that you have not come to cross-examine me again?"*
>
> *"No," Holmes answered, in his gentlest voice, "I will not cause you any unnecessary trouble, Lady Brackenstall, and my whole desire is to make things easy for you, for I am convinced that you are a much-tried woman. If you will treat me as a friend and trust me, you may find that I will justify your trust."[1]*

What Sherlock Holmes habitually lacks in tenderness or humility, he makes up for in loyalty and trust. He is reliable to a fault. This loyalty takes Sherlock Holmes, the two-dimensional character, and makes him three-dimensional. Sherlock Holmes becomes human in the eyes of his readers. The loyal Sherlock is a person, flawed without a doubt, yet worth salvaging, and even worth getting to know and learning to admire.

It is possible, without the addition of Dr. Watson, that there would be no Sherlock Holmes.

So it is for those who identify themselves as children of God.

Who could possibly imagine that Christ—perfect, holy, lovely—would be called *the friend of sinners*? History is plagued with people boasting unsavory qualities. Five minutes spent watching the evening news will reveal the unsavory Sherlock Holmes in every human heart. And yet Isaiah 53:5 tells one of the most amazing stories in the Bible: "But he was pierced for our transgressions; he was crushed for our iniquities; upon him was the chastisement that brought us peace, and with his wounds we are healed" (ESV).

Our friendship with Jesus Christ is the redeeming quality that takes our personality from unsavory to save-worthy. God's greatest gift to us is His own presence.

And once we form a friendship with God, we glorify Him best by trusting Him.

To be sure, David did not stand confidently in the Valley of Elah believing he was strong enough to kill a giant. One-hundred-year-old Abraham did not anticipate the birth of his son believing his wife could overcome her inability to bear children. Noah did not build an ark because of any vast experience with floods. These individuals, and scores of others like them, obeyed God for one reason: they trusted Him. And in trusting God, they found that He justified their trust.

> *Delight yourself in the LORD, and he will give you the desires of your heart. Commit your way to the LORD; trust in him, and he will act. He will bring forth your righteousness as the light, and your justice as the noonday.*
> PSALM 37:4–6 ESV

Notice the words *He will! He will! He will!*

Trusting God has little to do with understanding His motive and everything to do with obeying His will. This kind of trust leads to the only productive change in our lives. So obeying and trusting God are vitally connected. And the good news? No man has ever trusted God and found in the end that He is anything other than trustworthy.

John Calvin once said we must "never think it strange that He should gather to salvation those who have been the worst of men, and who have been covered with a mass of crimes."[2]

This is good news! We were once the worst of men and now we can be the children of God! Because of Jesus, we can form our own unlikely friendship with God.

*Trust in the L*ORD *with all your heart,*
and do not lean on your own understanding.
PROVERBS 3:5 ESV

5.

MEETING MYCROFT

"I confess that I have been blind as a mole, but it is
better to learn wisdom late than never to learn it at all."
THE MAN WITH THE TWISTED LIP

Dr. Watson opens "The Adventure of the Greek Interpreter" by talking about his relationship with Sherlock Holmes. In a blunt, almost comical manner, he describes Holmes as "an isolated phenomenon, a brain without a heart, and as deficient in human sympathy as he was preeminent in intelligence."[1]

Watson further describes Holmes' aversion to women and his unwillingness to form new friendships. Why anyone would love Sherlock Holmes after hearing him described this way is perhaps the biggest mystery of all in the canon. The paragraph concludes with Watson's admission: "But one day, to my very great surprise, [Holmes] began to talk to me about his brother."[2]

Sherlock Holmes has a brother?

And just like that, six years after Sherlock Holmes first appeared on the published page, we learn that he has an older brother named Mycroft. This admission—and the fact that he withheld it for so long—adds yet another layer of complexity to Holmes' already complicated personality.

So many questions arise. *Why did Holmes keep his brother a secret? Who is Mycroft? Where is he now?*

No one is more surprised about this revelation than Holmes' long-time roommate and friend, Dr. Watson, who had believed until now that Holmes was alone in the world. His response, "This was news to me indeed,"[3] would seem to be an understatement, though perhaps by this point, Watson had grown accustomed to the twists and turns of Holmes' bizarre inner workings.

Mycroft Holmes is only seen or heard from in four stories in the canon. He is described as being seven years older than Sherlock and possessing better deductive skills, though he is too lazy to bring cases to their conclusions. He is a government official who "won't even go out of his way to verify his own solutions, and he would rather be considered wrong than take the trouble to prove himself right."[4]

Life is full of surprises. Of this we can be certain.

Sometimes for the Christian, these surprises are good. God often provides for His children in unusual ways, for instance. Who doesn't love the story where, in a moment of desperation, God provided food for George Mueller's orphanage? How must the Israelites have felt when they took that first nerve-racking step into the Red Sea and discovered they were stepping on dry ground? We have a heavenly Father who takes delight in caring for His own. God will always meet us in our need.

God is our refuge and strength, a very present help in trouble. Therefore we will not fear though the earth gives way, though the mountains be moved into the heart of the sea, though its waters roar and foam, though the mountains tremble at its swelling.
PSALM 46:1–3 ESV

On the other hand, sometimes life's surprises are difficult. A cancer diagnosis, a car accident, or a broken relationship can send us into an emotional or spiritual tailspin.

In each of life's surprises, we find an equal opportunity to move forward or backward in our spiritual life. We can focus on the providence and forget the One who provided, or we can focus on the pain and forget the One who holds us in the palm of His hand.

Either way, focusing on anything other than God will yield frustrating results.

The road to Christlikeness is rough terrain. Where most of us would prefer a pilgrimage that cuts through pastures and winds around still waters, our earthly journey to heaven is filled with potholes and pitfalls. If our primary goal in this world is to be comfortable, then Christianity and the Word of God make no sense. With confidence befitting the Son of God, Jesus said to His beloved disciples, "I have said these things to you, that in me you may have peace. In the world you will have tribulation. But take heart; I have overcome the world" (John 16:33 ESV).

Thankfully, the surprises in life never defy the sovereignty of God. Comfort exists in the omnipotence of God because, with it, we can cling to the hope that God will work everything out for our good and His glory.

Even if our trials never make sense to us in this life, we can be certain they make sense to God. The tangles and knots we view from this vantage point will appear as a perfect work of art when studied from the perspective of heaven.

Our heavenly Father never promised an easy Christian life. In fact, Jesus said, "If anyone would come after me, let him deny himself and take up his cross and follow me. For whoever would save his life will lose it, but whoever loses his life for my sake will find it" (Matthew 16:24–25 ESV).

Instead of seeking relief from life's surprises, it is in our best interest to run hard after wisdom, remembering that the Lord of hosts is always with us. When we encounter the difficulties of this life—and we will—what we most need is not a therapist or a how-to book or a pro/con list (though these tools can be used by God to accomplish good in our lives). What we most need is God and His wisdom.

Life's surprises drive us beyond the range of our self-reliance. Though coming face-to-face with our weakness can be difficult at times, it is ultimately good because it forces us to lean hard on our heavenly Father.

We can take comfort in knowing the surprises in our life are never surprises to God.

Getting wisdom is the wisest thing you can do!
And whatever else you do, develop good judgment.
PROVERBS 4:7 NLT

6.

HOOKED

"Have a care! You can't play with edged tools forever without cutting those dainty hands."
THE ADVENTURE OF THE THREE GABLES

"The Adventure of the Three Gables" begins abruptly when a mysterious visitor shows up at the great detective's famous residence—221B Baker Street—and makes a strange demand: "See here, Mr. Holmes, you keep your hands out of other folks' business. Leave folks to manage their own affairs. Got that, [Mr.] Holmes?"[1]

The man, whom readers would soon discover is named Steve Dixie, insists that Sherlock Holmes stay away from a place called Harrow, specifically. And to be sure his point is understood, he swings a huge knotted lump of a fist under Sherlock Holmes' nose.

Nothing like an early morning threat to get a stubborn detective's blood pumping.

Dr. Watson, the narrator of the story, says, "If I had said that a mad bull had arrived, it would give a clearer impression of what occurred."[2]

All of this can only mean one thing: Sherlock Holmes is definitely going to get involved now. Warnings like the one delivered by Dixie always have the opposite effect on curious detectives who consider intimidation to be an invitation to play.

As soon as Dixie leaves, Holmes goes to work on his newest case. Of no surprise is the fact that strange things are happening at the following address: The Three Gables, Harrow Weald.

A story as exciting as any featuring the great detective unfolds.

"The Adventure of the Three Gables" is filled with many of the ingredients that make a good mystery: threats, eavesdropping, secrets, and surveillance. In what is not the first or last crime committed during his career, Holmes commits extortion before the story concludes in order to fund a trip around the world for an elderly, grieving woman who could not afford to go.

It would seem that Sherlock Holmes apparently borrowed a page from his predecessor, Robin Hood, who stole from the rich to give to the poor.

In the final paragraph of "The Adventure of the Three Gables," Holmes is talking to Isadora Klein, a wealthy, beautiful woman who resorted to manipulation and deception to get what she wanted, and the detective utters the famous line: "Have a care! Have a care! You can't play with edged tools forever without cutting those dainty hands."[3]

Edged tools, in this case, did not refer to any literal sharp or dangerous object. Isadora Klein wasn't playing with knives or brandishing swords. Instead, *edged tools* referred to the woman's poor choices. Holmes was sending a warning of sorts to a woman who was accustomed to getting her way by relying on choices that were sketchy at best and criminal at worst.

In this case, Holmes' language is consistent with the words of scripture. "Can a man walk on hot coals without his feet being scorched?" (Proverbs 6:28 NIV) Proverbs' *hot coals* and Klein's *edged tools* are one and the same.

Never in the Bible is sin taken lightly. We are never encouraged to wink at bad habits or poke fun at transgressions. Scripture never offers psychological or genetic justification for our poor choices. And yet we have a horrible tendency to minimize our own sin. We are prone to indulge in self-pity, for example, or cling to the pitfalls of pride and praise. Bitterness and envy don't look that bad, after all, when held up next to murder or blasphemy.

And yet all sin—every choice we make that is contrary to the nature of God—springs from our beliefs and demonstrates that our heart is in danger. We should be troubled to our core that we love and nurture the things for which Jesus died.

We ought to say with the psalmist:

Wash me thoroughly from my iniquity, and cleanse me

from my sin! For I know my transgressions, and my sin
is ever before me. Against you, you only,
have I sinned and done what is evil in your sight.
PSALM 51:2–4 ESV

The problem with sin is that we forget the goodness of God in our rush to create our own definition of what is good. This was the problem with man's first sin and every sin since. God instructs us to love other people, and yet we believe it would be better to pick and choose who deserves our kind affection. God commands us to pray without ceasing, yet we think it would be easier to work out our own solutions. God tells us to trust Him, yet we choose instead to worry.

We should diligently guard our hearts and lives from sinful choices, however large or small, that threaten to destroy our relationship with the Almighty.

To use the imagery of Sherlock Holmes, our poor choices are like edged tools. We may be able to dabble with them for a time without experiencing the agonizing consequences, but eventually we will cut our hands, and the scars will be long lasting.

Can a man scoop a flame into his
lap and not have his clothes catch on fire?
PROVERBS 6:27 NLT

7.

GAME OF PROOF

"The temptation to form premature theories upon insufficient data is the bane of our profession."
THE VALLEY OF FEAR

Nothing gets past Sherlock Holmes.

Throughout the canon, the mastermind detective is portrayed as a great lover of deduction. In many of the stories, he can be found at the scene of a crime with a magnifying glass in one hand and a seemingly insignificant object in the other. He loves fingerprint evidence and can distinguish the tiny inconsistencies between the print of various typewriters. He solved "The Boscombe Valley Mystery" using footprint analyses almost exclusively.

For Sherlock Holmes, the smaller the clue, the greater the challenge.

Once he returns to his beloved 221B Baker Street apartment after visiting a crime scene, he carefully sifts through the evidence, looking for the slightest deviation or indication of who committed the crime.

When talking to clients or companions, Holmes often stresses the need to safeguard the integrity of the evidence. In fact, Holmes is the first detective—fictional or otherwise—ever to protect crime scenes from contamination. Holmes' reverence for and careful treatment of evidence at the crime scene is one of his most valuable gifts to the world.

Why does evidence matter so much? Forensic evidence, in the mind of the master detective, is the only part of a case that does not lie. Everyone involved in a crime has an agenda, good or bad. The prosecutor wants justice. The defense wants guiltlessness. The accused wants freedom.

The evidence wants nothing.

More than once in the canon, Holmes says to Watson, "When you have eliminated the impossible, whatever remains, however improbable, must be the truth."[1]

Christians would do well to apply this type of logic to identifying fools.

The Bible—and in particular the book of Proverbs—spends a great deal of time listing the characteristics of a fool.

Fools despise wisdom and instruction (see Proverbs 1:7).
The mouth of a fool brings ruin (see Proverbs 10:14).
Fools take no pleasure in understanding
  (see Proverbs 18:2).

The list of biblical evidence for recognizing fools is long and unambiguous. Fools hate knowledge, display apathy, act recklessly, speak sloppily, and respond angrily. They cannot handle instruction, regardless of who gives it, and they often hurt the people who love them the most.

And yet we can be quick to defend or justify them, can't we? It isn't socially savvy to deal harshly with someone on the basis of his or her life choices. "To each his own" has become the mantra of our culture, and all too often, even within the church. "I've watched him grow up!" or "She has a good heart!" can replace the type of urgent concern we should have for someone who is acting like a fool. Why does foolishness matter? Fools have great capacity to ruin their lives and the lives of those around them. "There is a way that seems right to a man, but its end is the way to death" (Proverbs 14:12 ESV).

We can always assume God has a good reason behind every command.

Fools, like criminals, are hard pressed to cover the evidence at the end of the day. While it is possible to temporarily demonstrate a contradiction between actions and beliefs, it is impossible to hide the truth forever. Eventually, the evidence—foolishness in the heart—will speak for itself. Genuine repentance and faith in God, after all, is not content with lip service.

It should be noted that sinning is not the mark of a fool— everyone sins. Being uncorrectable is the mark of a fool.

For we ourselves were once foolish, disobedient,
led astray, slaves to various passions and pleasures,
passing our days in malice and envy, hated by others and

*hating one another. But when the goodness and loving
kindness of God our Savior appeared, he saved us,
not because of works done by us in righteousness,
but according to his own mercy.*
TITUS 3:3–5 ESV

Recognizing and responding appropriately to fools is of critical importance because no one who loves God and His Word will remain indifferent to someone who doesn't. Shrugging off a fool or making excuses for his choices is a dangerous step toward becoming a fool. At the same time, engaging a fool in a foolish way is not wise. The challenge is to admonish a fool without adopting his methods or tactics. This task can be easier said than done.

No child of God should want to be categorized as a fool.

The bottom line is, when God gives us new birth, we display unmistakable evidence of new life. Doing good works doesn't save us, but good works demonstrate to others that we are saved. It should not take a forensic scientist to come to the conclusion that we love God and want to pursue His wisdom for our lives.

*The way of fools seems right to them,
but the wise listen to advice.*
PROVERBS 12:15 NIV

8.

THE POWER OF RESTRAINT

"I had grasped the significance of the silence of the dog,
for one true inference invariably suggests others."
SILVER BLAZE

"Silver Blaze" is one of Conan Doyle's most popular short stories and one of the most famous sporting mysteries ever written.

In it, Holmes is asked to investigate the disappearance of a famous racehorse on the eve of a significant race. And if that weren't enough drama for one story, it would also appear that the horse's trainer, John Straker, has been murdered.

Holmes will employ some of his best observations ever recorded to solve this crime.

In "Silver Blaze," Holmes makes a statement that has been repeated often in other literary works. The Inspector asks Holmes, "Is there any other point to which you would wish to draw my attention?" and the following exchange ensues:

"To the curious incident of the dog in the night-time,"
[answers Holmes].
"The dog did nothing in the night-time."
"That was the curious incident."[1]

This conversation is so popular that it has been parodied in books, movies, and television. Published works have even been titled *The Curious Incident of the Dog in the Night Time.*

One detective writer and Sherlock Holmes enthusiast, Monsignor Ronald Knox, coined the phrase "Sherlockismus" for this type of quick-witted banter for which Sherlock Holmes is famous. According to Knox, Holmes utters as many as 173 examples of *Sherlockismus.*[2]

In "Silver Blaze," Sherlock Holmes solves the crime of the horse and trainer as much because of what he does *not* see as what he *does* observe.

Often, what isn't said or done matters as much as what actually happens.

Arriving at good theological conclusions about God and life depends on seeing what is *not* in the Bible as much as recognizing what *is* in the Word of God.

For instance, we know that God is love. The Bible is replete with verses that support this truth.

> *Beloved, let us love one another, for love is from God, and whoever loves has been born of God and knows God. Anyone who does not love does not know God, because God is love.*
> I JOHN 4:7–8 ESV

So we have come to know and to believe the love

that God has for us. God is love, and whoever
abides in love abides in God, and God abides in him.
1 JOHN 4:16 ESV

And yet, a careful reading of these verses does not say that God loves people to the point of excusing sin or overlooking faithlessness—quite the opposite. Many other verses in the Bible speak to God's righteous standard and the requirement for faith in order to live eternally with Him in heaven. What we do not see in scripture is that God overlooks sin.

It has been said that John 3:16 was once the most well-known verse in the Bible, but now the title belongs to another verse: "Judge not, that you be not judged" (Matthew 7:1 ESV).

Believers and nonbelievers alike use this verse to defend themselves against people who would point out egregious error or bad judgment in their lives. Yet we know scripture encourages accountability and even admonishes believers to rebuke each other in love. So what the verse says in context is as important as what it does not say. In the case of Matthew 7:1, we should provoke each other to good works while, at the same time, refraining from a judgmental attitude that would repel relationship.

We do not see any admonition to condone wrongdoing.

Sometimes we are tempted to read the Bible for what we want it to say instead of what it actually says. For instance, the Bible never instructs us to hate sinners. We should hate sin—

no question about it—but God commands us to love our neighbors without any indication that the neighbors must be believers in order to be recipients of our kind deeds.

Some writers jokingly refer to misused passages as *butchered Bible verses*, but despite this catchy title, a serious problem exists. When we read things in the Bible that aren't actually there, we risk constructing a faulty faith or worshipping our own viewpoint as god.

God commissioned Joshua in the Old Testament with these words, and we would do well to apply them to our lives:

> *"This Book of the Law shall not depart from your mouth,*
> *but you shall meditate on it day and night, so that you*
> *may be careful to do according to all that is written in it.*
> *For then you will make your way prosperous, and then*
> *you will have good success."*
> JOSHUA 1:8 ESV

Just as we wouldn't justify placing a little arsenic in a child's bottle—*It's just a little! What could it hurt?*—we should never rationalize adding a little of our own opinion to the Word of God. We should be diligent to ensure that God's opinions instruct our own.

As children of God, we must be committed to recognizing what isn't in the Bible as readily as we see what is. The stronger our theology, the deeper our faith will be, and the deeper our faith is, the more useful we will be to God.

We must pray that God gives us sound discernment as we study.

Forever, O LORD, Your word is settled in heaven.
PSALM 119:89 NKJV

9.

OBSERVATION SKILLS

"This is a time for observation, not for talk."
THE ADVENTURE OF THE RED-HEADED LEAGUE

Sherlock Holmes popularized the steps of the scientific process.

A careful study of each story featuring the detective will reveal that he followed a consistent pattern: state the problem, conduct research, formulate a hypothesis, test the hypothesis, and confirm or deny the theory. Sometimes—although not often—Holmes finished the process only to begin again due to a faulty original hypothesis.

In "The Adventure of the Red-Headed League"—which happens to be Conan Doyle's second favorite story featuring Sherlock Holmes—a London pawnbroker named Jabez Wilson consults Holmes and Watson. Wilson, most noted for his blazing red hair, believes he may have been the brunt of a practical joke, and he wants Holmes to get to the bottom of it.

Holmes, believing the mystery to be "refreshingly unusual,"[1] agrees to take the case, and eventually Wilson goes on his way to let the great detective begin his work. As soon as Wilson leaves, Holmes promptly curls up in his chair, draws his knees up to his nose, and smokes three pipes in fifty minutes.

Side note: one Sherlock Holmes devotee wrote that smoking three pipes in fifty minutes "was not a feat—it was a monstrous abuse of the membrane of the nose and throat!"[2] He was right.

Holmes became so still in his chair that Dr. Watson became convinced the detective had fallen asleep. Then, all of a sudden, Holmes sprang from his chair and asked Watson to accompany him to a concert. *A concert? In the middle of a case?* Together, Holmes and Watson set off for the concert hall, Holmes thumping his walking stick on the pavement as they traveled.

What must have looked like two average men just taking a walk on an ordinary day was actually Holmes employing his scientific method.

State the problem, conduct research, formulate a hypothesis, test the hypothesis, and confirm or deny the theory.

Little did Watson understand that every step between 221B Baker Street and St. James Hall, where the concert was to be held, was carefully calculated by Holmes who was silently gathering evidence and testing theories. At one point, Watson starts asking Holmes a series of questions and Holmes answers:

"My dear doctor, this is a time for observation, not

for talk. We are spies in an enemy's country. We know
something of Saxe-Coburg Square. Let us now explore
the parts which lie behind it."[3]

Unintentionally, Holmes offered Watson a biblical solution to an ordinary problem.

Often when faced with a perplexing situation, we are, by nature, more interested in jumping to a conclusion or placing the guilt than we are putting in the time and effort to uncover the underlying issues. It is generally more enjoyable, after all, to discuss motives than to go to the source and ask questions, isn't it? Especially if we are in any way perpetuating the trouble.

We are all at risk of becoming hopelessly self-absorbed, especially during seasons of hurt or frustration. *How could they do that? Why did she say that? Why me?*

Sometimes when trouble comes, the best thing we can do in lieu of hunting down answers is to be quiet and observe.

To be certain, listening carefully isn't always the easiest inclination. Sometimes we'd prefer to insert unsolicited opinions or become distracted by thoughts of a response while someone is speaking. We hear about an offense and rush to pin the fault on someone or assume the emotions of the person who is talking to us or telling us the story. Instead, we should remind ourselves of the detective's words: "This is a time for observation, not for talk," and we should carefully, scientifically gather the evidence. "Know this, my beloved brothers: let every person be quick to hear, slow to speak, slow to anger; for the anger of man does not produce the righteousness of God" (James 1:19–20 ESV).

Though Holmes was a fictional detective who applied the steps of the scientific process to crime, it is a good idea to apply the same type of careful precision to life.

State the problem, conduct research, formulate a hypothesis, test the hypothesis, and confirm or deny the idea.

And every step we take—each word and action—should be covered in prayer, asking God to do for us what we are incapable of doing for ourselves. It is His wisdom and not our own that should govern our dealings with others. "Above all, keep loving one another earnestly, since love covers a multitude of sins" (1 Peter 4:8 ESV).

Apologies could be spared and relationships could be saved if we learned to delay our conclusions until the right amount of investigation has been done.

The author of Proverbs understands the default response of humanity because time and again he encourages us to think before we speak and to apply due diligence to a matter before we answer. Wisdom—which is what Proverbs aims to persuade us to pursue—is living in light of God's design and looking at life from the perspective of our heavenly Father.

We would do well to heed the advice.

Spouting off before listening to the
facts is both shameful and foolish.

PROVERBS 18:13 NLT

10.

HOME SWEET HOLMES

"So it was, my dear Watson, that at two o'clock to-day
I found myself in my old armchair in my own old room,
and only wishing that I could have seen my old friend
Watson in the other chair which he has so often adorned."

THE ADVENTURE OF THE EMPTY HOUSE

"The Adventure of the Empty House" is perhaps the most applauded story in the canon. It was the first story published after Sherlock Holmes' death in "The Final Problem."

The Strand Magazine, which published the stories that made Sherlock Holmes a sensation, wanted the forgiveness—or perhaps, more specifically, the restored subscription base—of its disgruntled readers. They plastered the words "The Return of Sherlock Holmes" in thick, bold letters above the title of Conan Doyle's first published story ten years after Holmes died.

And it worked.

Just as suspected, readers were quick to forgive the magazine—and specifically their beloved detective—and allow both back into their good graces. Life resumed, and the story picked up where it left off ten years later with "The Adventure of the Empty House."

In this short story, Holmes is explaining the circumstances around his fake death and subsequent disappearance to his dear friend Watson when he says:

> *"So it was, my dear Watson, that at two o'clock to-*
> *day I found myself in my old armchair in my own old*
> *room, and only wishing that I could have seen my old*
> *friend Watson in the other chair which he has so often*
> *adorned."*[1]

Perhaps those were the words Dr. Watson most needed to hear since, soon enough, the pair went on their way solving London's most terrifying crimes, all traces of the ten-year gap in their relationship vanished in the air along with the smoke from Sherlock's notorious pipe.

True students of the mastermind recommend that readers enjoy the entire canon twice—once to experience the thrill of solving the mysteries and once to witness the remarkable friendship between the detective and his assistant. For in addition to the carefully crafted crime scenes, Conan Doyle paints a portrait of two friends enjoying each other's company in a simple apartment on Baker Street.

One of the reasons people are willing to overlook Holmes' general social pitfalls is because of the human element represented in his relationship to Dr. Watson. In "The Adventure of the Empty House," even after an entire decade of not speaking to each other, the relationship between Holmes and Watson is quickly and entirely restored. Perhaps this fact rings true for readers because, as anyone with an age-long friendship understands, it is entirely possible to live apart without growing apart.

Truth: Sherlock Holmes found more of a friend in Dr. Watson than he ever did in his own brother, Mycroft.

We, too, have a Friend who sticks closer than a brother.

John Bunyan, the author of *Pilgrim's Progress,* who was writing two hundred years before Arthur Conan Doyle, said: "And, indeed, this is one of the greatest mysteries in the world; namely, that a righteousness that resides in heaven should justify me, a sinner on earth!"[2]

Another of God's great mysteries is that He adopted us in addition to justifying us. These actions are separate and undeniable gifts. Neither is deserved, but both are extraordinary.

We—because of salvation through Jesus Christ—can be the friend of God. Because of the work on the cross, we can talk to God and He will listen. Even after long stretches of silence on our part, when our heavenly Father should willingly wash His hands of us, He stands ready to pardon and restore if we seek His forgiveness. When we enter His presence, He makes our pleas and prayers a priority. Never are we told to wait or instructed to come back at a more convenient time. "Call to me and I will answer you, and will tell you great and hidden things that you have not known" (Jeremiah 33:3 ESV).

Important to note: it was in Sherlock Holmes' power to restore his relationship with Dr. Watson at any time. Theories abound as to why it took him so long to make the first move, but the truth remains. Holmes—not Dr. Watson—was responsible for the gap in communication.

And so it is with us.

When we feel far from God, it is not God who has ceased the communication with us.

Unlike our earthly friends who are distracted by the mundane challenges of everyday existence, God is always ready and willing to listen and restore. "The LORD is near to all who call on him, to all who call on him in truth" (Psalm 145:18 ESV).

The glorious reality is that God's availability knows no difference between Sunday evening services and Monday morning car line. It doesn't matter if we pray to Him while kneeling at an altar or while pillowing our head to sleep. We are invited—commanded—to approach Him at all times about all things. This is a privilege of the highest kind. We do not have that kind of accessibility to anyone else.

But if that is not enough, God graciously gives us tangible evidences of His presence in the form of Christian companions with whom to enjoy life. As children of God, we are blessed beyond measure.

A man of many companions may come to ruin,
but there is a friend who sticks closer than a brother.
PROVERBS 18:24 ESV

11.

A STUDY IN SILENCE

"You have a grand gift for silence, Watson.
It makes you quite invaluable as a companion."
THE MAN WITH THE TWISTED LIP

One characteristic of many that separated Sherlock Holmes and Dr. Watson was their willingness or unwillingness to share personal opinions at inappropriate times.

For instance, where Holmes disliked most forms of authority and took regular opportunity to ruffle the feathers of the Scotland Yard, Dr. Watson, on the other hand, maintained a healthy appreciation for keeping his personal opinions to a minimum.

Bottom line, Dr. Watson was generally better at keeping his mouth closed when necessary.

Holmes would, no doubt, have found himself in much more trouble over the course of his career had it not been for the quieting influence of his dear friend and companion.

As the plot goes, Dr. Watson married Mary Morstan who was first introduced in *The Sign of Four*. She is mentioned only briefly in a few stories before she dies of a cause not named in the canon. While married to Morstan, Watson doesn't live at 221B Baker Street.

Late one night, Dr. Watson received a frantic visit from a friend of his wife. The woman's husband was missing—gone for several days—and the woman was concerned that he was caught in a dangerous drug binge. Desperate for help, the woman asked Dr. Watson to help her bring her husband home.

And so "The Man with the Twisted Lip" opens in a well-known opium den in crime-riddled East London. Interesting to note, when the story was published in 1891, selling opium was not a crime. The activity was linked to criminals and was viewed as objectionable by respectable society, but the drug use was done openly and without legal consequences.

Dr. Watson, who is known as much for his sense of loyalty as Sherlock Holmes is known for his skills of deduction, agreed to help his wife's friend find her husband. Once they arrive at the opium den, however, Watson makes an incredible discovery. In his own words:

> *I felt a sudden pluck at my skirt, and a low voice whispered, "Walk past me, and then look back at me."*
> *The words fell quite distinctly upon my ear. I glanced down. They could only have come from the old man at my side, and yet he sat now as absorbed as ever, very thin, very wrinkled, bent with age. . . I took two steps forward and looked back. . . . There, sitting by the fire and grinning at my surprise, was none other than Sherlock Holmes.[1]*

Holmes—disguised as an old man—was extracting information from a visitor to the opium den.

And that quickly, a new adventure with multiple layers is born.

At one point in "The Man with the Twisted Lip," when Watson and Holmes are riding in an open one-horse vehicle, Holmes says something to Watson that sums up the strength of their relationship. "You have a grand gift for silence, Watson. It makes you quite invaluable as a companion."[2]

He was right, of course. Dr. Watson knew when to ask questions and when to be quiet.

Sometimes keeping our mouth shut is the wisest thing we can do. Silence—not speaking—is usually the better trademark of wisdom.

No one understands this better than Job, whose friends were a comfort to him until they opened their mouths. "And they sat with him on the ground seven days and seven nights, and no one spoke a word to him, for they saw that his suffering was very great" (Job 2:13 ESV).

Had Job's friends kept their mouths closed, history might have left them a different legacy. Today, comparing someone to "one of Job's friends" is no compliment.

James 1:19 admonishes us to "be quick to hear [and] slow to speak" (ESV). And while at first glance this seems like an easy task, sometimes it is the hardest job of all. God would not speak so often of our need to be quiet if it were the natural thing to do. Instead, the Bible is filled with examples of when saying the wrong thing at the wrong time brought grim consequences.

Consider Adam's response when he was caught in the first sin or Zechariah, who lost all ability to speak until his son John was born. Abraham, in a moment of panic, risked his marriage and placed innocent lives in danger when he introduced Sarah as his sister.

On the flip side, consider Christ's response when He was persecuted:

> *He was oppressed, and he was afflicted, yet he*
> *opened not his mouth; like a lamb that is led to*
> *the slaughter, and like a sheep that before its*
> *shearers is silent, so he opened not his mouth.*
> ISAIAH 53:7 ESV

Christ's silence is of great significance to the story of the cross. At no other time in human history has anyone ever had more of a right to open his mouth and vindicate his reputation, and yet Christ said nothing.

Christ's silence is humility personified. Christ's silence should motivate our own.

One reason that it matters so much how we respond to other people—whether we are quick to speak or slow to hear—is because, typically, the way we interact with people reflects the way we interact with our heavenly Father. If we habitually defend ourselves or offer excuses for our failures, for instance, chances are we do the same thing with God. Difficulty listening to people in general likely illustrates a problem with listening to God.

We should strive to listen well.

And since our words are the most tangible evidence of what is happening in our heart, it is essential that we learn to control them by aligning our desires with the desires of God.

Watch your tongue and keep your mouth shut,
and you will stay out of trouble.
PROVERBS 21:23 NLT

12.

THE ART OF DEDUCTION

"It is stupidity rather than courage to refuse
to recognize danger when it is close upon you."
THE FINAL PROBLEM

Without Sherlock Holmes, forensic science as we know it would not exist.

Known for his intellectual genius and astonishing skills of deduction, Holmes—or perhaps more to the point, Conan Doyle—created methods that are still used in police and detective agencies around the world. Holmes is cited in academic journals, while entire forensic science classes utilize the great detective as their model for employing the scientific method.

Holmes employed forensic methods throughout the canon. In many ways, he was 120 years ahead of his time, making him both fascinating and timeless. He was the first to utilize bullet trajectory as criminal evidence, for instance, and he was the first to employ scientific evaluation to detect the presence of poison.

When Holmes burst onto the scene in Victorian England, the police and detectives of the nineteenth century did not know about forensic science. Their job was to move bodies and interview witnesses. More cases ended up cold than solved.

The police of Victorian England have been described as *all brawn and no brain*. They were overworked and underpaid. Police work was considered entry-level employment and was given to men with little to no training or experience. Because of this, innocent people were sometimes blamed. At other times, crimes simply went unsolved.

Very little attention was given to the actual scene of the crime. Valuable evidence was trampled over or totally disregarded. Police of the day might have asked, "Who cares about a random button on the floor or some blood splatter on the ceiling? What does that have to do with identifying the criminal?"

Enter Sherlock Holmes, who believed every item at a crime scene could be evidence.

Conan Doyle created a multidimensional character who cared as much—or likely more—about the evidence as he did the victim, and everything about crime solving changed. It has been said that when Conan Doyle published his first novel, *A Study in Scarlet*, he unknowingly issued the first manual on forensic science. This is an incredible accomplishment for a work of literature.

Even more extraordinary, Sherlock Holmes is still solving crimes in the form of the methods he used in his adventures.

As Christians, we could take a page from Holmes' manual

on observation and deduction. As children of God in a culture that is not kind to Christianity, it is paramount that we learn to be discerning.

The apostle Paul, having heard discouraging and disturbing news about a church that he had planted, wrote a letter urging the believers to live for God. In his final instructions he wrote: "Be watchful, stand firm in the faith, act like men, be strong" (1 Corinthians 16:13 ESV). This, of course, is still good advice for the church in the twenty-first century.

Much of the world does not want to see us successful in our Christian life. Certain pockets of nonbelievers work overtime to trip us up or put us down. The devil and those who serve him want nothing more than to destroy our walk and witness. And sometimes, if we're honest, we make it easy for them to accomplish their mission.

Every day we are told things about ourselves and about our Savior that are incorrect. We hear things on television shows or in song lyrics. We observe things in public or think things in private. We are flooded with communication—much of which is incompatible with what we know to be true from scripture. Many of us hear as much or more in a given day that disagrees with God's truth than agrees with it.

What we do with this wrong information makes all the difference.

The undiscerning child of God is ricocheted in his choices and convictions like a pinball—bouncing from worldview to worldview—while the discerning believer is anchored to the truth of God, unwilling to budge in the heat of the moment.

In the words of the New Testament, we should make steadfastness in God our aim— "So that we may no longer be children, tossed to and fro by the waves and carried about by every wind of doctrine, by human cunning, by craftiness in deceitful schemes" (Ephesians 4:14 ESV).

We are arrogant if we believe we can expose ourselves to endless human wisdom without employing careful discrimination and not be affected by it. Salvation alone does not make us immune to falling victim to unbiblical thinking and living.

At the heart of observation and deduction is God's wisdom.

There is a vast difference between wisdom and intelligence. Smart people make a mess of their lives all the time. Sherlock Holmes exemplified this with his occasional drug binges and in-home target practice. He was smart, but he wasn't always wise. In the age of the Internet, it is possible to acquire knowledge on virtually any topic with a click of a button, but God's wisdom must be developed in an altogether different, more disciplined way—"The fear of the LORD is the beginning of wisdom, and the knowledge of the Holy One is insight" (Proverbs 9:10 ESV).

True wisdom is found in the Word of God, which means if we want to be wise, we must apply ourselves to study and meditation—actively occupying our mind on the truths of God—so we can recognize danger when it is close upon us.

The prudent sees danger and hides himself,
but the simple go on and suffer for it.
PROVERBS 22:3 ESV

13.

THE POWER OF POSSIBILITY

"It is, I admit, mere imagination; but how often is imagination the mother of truth?"
THE VALLEY OF FEAR

Sherlock Holmes is bigger than the stories in which he appears.

Need evidence of this? Add a deerstalker hat and a pipe to a stick figure and the illustration will be instantly recognizable. Even people who have never read the stories of Sherlock Holmes know basic facts about the great detective and can recognize him if given the opportunity.

Holmes has experienced more popularity over the span of a century than any other fictional character. He now appears in more stories written by people other than Arthur Conan Doyle than he did in the original sixty by the original author. Hundreds of stories are still being published each year with Holmes as the central character.

These noncanonical Sherlock Holmes stories fall into one of four broad categories: new stories about Holmes, stories in which Holmes plays a supporting role but is not the central character, stories about descendants of Holmes, and stories inspired by, but not including, Holmes.

People who either really love the great detective or want to grasp the coattails of Conan Doyle's success create spin-offs involving Holmes that sell thousands of copies to die-hard Holmes fans. The world cannot get enough of the great detective.

One author wrote a story in which Professor Moriarty was actually Jack the Ripper. Another author sent Holmes to Brazil to solve the case of the missing Stradivarius violin. Still another author wrote a six-book series in which Holmes solves crimes in Minnesota.

Very few literary characters have successfully lived independent of the story in which they were written. Holmes is not only recognizable to people who have never read the stories, but Holmes exists in other authors' works, transcending his own story world. In many ways, Holmes is a literary and cultural marvel.

This incredible success is partly to blame for the many readers who choose to believe Holmes is still alive in the twenty-first century and is solving crimes somewhere in the world.

Perhaps what this really proves is that readers believe what they want to believe. Christians do, too.

Through the use of our imaginations, we are capable of creating story worlds that transcend reality. Maybe we believe someone is mad at us, or we think we know someone's motives. Perhaps we fear the loss of health even while living healthy lives, or we worry about losing our home or job even while God continues to meet every one of our needs. There are millions of things to worry about, and some of us are skilled enough to worry about it all.

The problem is that all worry reflects a shift in trust.

We cannot worry and actively believe verses like "For I know the plans I have for you, declares the LORD, plans for welfare and not for evil, to give you a future and a hope" (Jeremiah 29:11 ESV).

Fear can feel as factual as reality. Tragic *what-if*s dominate our thinking and control our choices. Some of us live through a difficult circumstance one hundred times before it happens—if it happens at all. We become so worked up thinking about a possibility that we experience the emotions as if the difficulty actually occurred.

Make no mistake, living in a sin-cursed culture means we are surrounded by people and ideals that legitimately strike fear into our hearts. Reading about terrorist organizations whose chief goal it is to wipe Christians off the face of the earth isn't a recipe for indifference. Hearing about a disease that has the power to kill millions doesn't lend itself naturally to calm.

Which is why we must filter everything we think about through promises like "Cast your cares on the LORD and he will sustain you; he will never let the righteous be shaken" (Psalm 55:22 NIV).

We are only ever shaken when we choose to worry instead of trust.

We can overcome our worst fears because God is bigger than the stories in which He appears. No promise of God is too good to be true.

Trust in God is the only solution that can unshackle us from fears that would ultimately destroy us. The truth is, we write our own stories every day by what we think. Do we believe that God is more powerful than our worst fears? What we choose to imagine says as much about what we believe as anything else.

To combat fear, everything in our lives must be adjusted to the truth of God's Word. "Even though I walk through the valley of the shadow of death, I will fear no evil, for you are with me" (Psalm 23:4 ESV).

If the psalmist could commit to trusting God while walking through the valley of the shadow of death, certainly we can trust God on days when our worst concerns are merely imaginary.

We must remember that we are not given the grace to experience imaginary events, but we can take comfort in the reality that God's grace will be there if and when we need it for actual events.

And since we have the power to choose what we imagine, we should choose to visualize our lives under the sovereign control of God. We should never imagine a worst-case scenario apart from the hope that comes from knowing Him.

It isn't enough to decide, "I am not going to be afraid." This type of exercise is futile. Our imagination has been overwhelmed by something big and terrifying. We must overcome our fear by thinking bigger, truer, nobler thoughts about something big enough to overcome what concerns us. We must think better thoughts about God.

It has rightly been said that all fear is a form of imagination.

So imagine better!

> *For as he thinketh in his heart, so is he.*
> PROVERBS 23:7 KJV

AGE OF REASON

*"Watson, if it should ever strike you that I am getting
a little over-confident in my powers, kindly whisper,
'Norbury' in my ear, and I shall be infinitely obliged to you."*
THE ADVENTURE OF THE YELLOW FACE

Based on the way Sherlock Holmes and Dr. Watson are sometimes portrayed in plays, sitcoms, and movies, it is easy to think of them as stuffy, middle-aged detectives with impressive careers and immeasurable wisdom.

In reality, the pair was only in their twenties when they met and began solving the crimes that would make them famous. They were anything but stuffy, middle-aged, or wise.

In "The Adventure of the Veiled Lodger," we learn that Sherlock's career as a detective lasted twenty-three years, with Watson working alongside him for seventeen of them. In this unlikely pair, each would become incomplete without the other.

Because they were both intelligent—Sherlock proficient in deduction and Watson skilled in medicine—they were able to push each other to be better at everything they did.

Side note: in only two stories involving Sherlock Holmes is no murder committed. "The Adventure of the Yellow Face" is one of those stories. This short story is particularly interesting because it involves minimal detection and no crime. And yet, in a stunning twist, Holmes comes to the wrong conclusion about the case. The overly confident detective finds himself facing his own limitations in a small cottage in Norbury.

Thankfully, Arthur Conan Doyle believed in the importance of a positive ending and everything worked out by the last page, but for a few helpless moments, fans of Holmes are left slack-jawed as the detective reels. In the last lines of the story, where we would normally watch a confident Holmes prove he was right all along, instead we see an unusually humbled detective. Watson writes:

> *Not another word did he say of the case until late that night when he was turning away, with his lighted candle, for his bedroom. "Watson," said he, "if it should ever strike you that I am getting a little over-confident in my powers, kindly whisper, 'Norbury' in my ear, and I shall be infinitely obliged to you."*[1]

This unprecedented modesty in Holmes is insightful.

We would all do well to have a Dr. Watson who could whisper reminders in our ear of our own shortcomings when we become too confident in our abilities. We like to think that our choicest friends are the ones who enrich us with positive affirmations and motivations about ourselves, but in reality, our most valuable friends are the ones who know when to cheer us and when to admonish us.

The right kind of friend will do both. "Listen to advice and accept instruction, that you may gain wisdom in the future" (Proverbs 19:20 ESV).

Christian friendship, by definition, should strengthen our character and improve our relationship with God. Any Christian friendship that does not meet these qualifications should come under our careful scrutiny.

One of the great gifts in the Bible is the glimpse we are given into historical friendships—both good and bad. We can observe the blessings of friendship from Jonathan and David, Ruth and Naomi, and Daniel, Shadrach, Meshach, and Abednego, for instance. On the other hand, we can heed the warnings from Job and his friends or Abraham and Lot.

The fact that God inspired the writers of scripture to include practical stories of helpful and harmful relationships is invaluable because we can trace a line from their choices to their consequences. We can observe the opportunities that various biblical characters took or missed to whisper, "Norbury" in the ear of their friends. The humility that Jonathan showed David, for example, is just as insightful as the unrestraint demonstrated by Lot toward Abraham.

Good friendships are good for us, and—if they are stewarded—they are good for testimony. "By this all people will know that you are my disciples, if you have love for one another" (John 13:35 ESV).

Sometimes what we most need is a friend who can remind us of the unfailing goodness of God as seen in the past events of our lives. At other times, we need a friend to reprove and rebuke us in our pride. Building Christian relationships that stand the test of time enables us to invest in each other's lives in a deep and meaningful way. But this type of relationship building isn't easy. It requires intentionality and pursuit that extends beyond casual contact over social media or a brief "hello" in the hallway at church.

This type of friendship requires a conversation much like the one Holmes had with Watson on the night he failed his case. We need to establish friendships in which we can talk openly and honestly about what it means to admonish each other in the Lord.

As often as possible, Christian friends should pray together, fellowship together, worship together, and serve together, looking for opportunities to sharpen each other as God intended.

Good Christian friends are vastly important for our walk with God. More than just a dinner date or a listening ear, the right kind of Christian friend will become a co-pilgrim in the Christian journey, willing to encourage or rebuke us along the way. God often uses good, believing friends as instruments of grace and sanctification in our lives.

We are familiar with the verse that talks about the faithful wounds of a friend, but less familiar is the verse before it: "Better is open rebuke than hidden love" (Proverbs 27:5 ESV).

The benefits that accompany Christian friendship are one reason to pursue long-term, iron-sharpening-iron relationships in the body of Christ for the glory of God.

> *Wounds from a sincere friend are*
> *better than many kisses from an enemy.*
> PROVERBS 27:6 NLT

15.

THE MAIL MAYHEM

*"Nothing clears up a case so much
as stating it to another person."*
SILVER BLAZE

In "Silver Blaze," Sherlock Holmes is investigating the case of the stolen racehorse and the murdered trainer when he decides to fill Dr. Watson in on the details of the case. According to Watson: "Holmes, leaning forward, with his long, thin forefinger checking off the points upon the palm of his left hand, gave me a sketch of the events which had led to our journey."[1]

You can see it, can't you? Sherlock Holmes, tall and thin with piercing eyes and nervous fingers, carefully recounting the details of the case for his friend, Dr. Watson. According to the canon, this was a familiar scene. But why would Sherlock Holmes—better at solving crimes than anyone else—spend so much time rehearsing the case with Dr. Watson?

The answer is simple. Research shows that the best way to learn or understand something is to communicate it to someone else.

Throughout the canon, Dr. Watson serves as Holmes'

assistant, biographer, friend, and flatmate, but he also functions as a sort of sounding board for the great detective. Holmes often explains his choices to Watson, teaching him and even criticizing him when he doesn't feel the doctor has figured something out quickly enough or paid enough attention.

Which happens frequently.

One of Holmes' best backhanded compliments to Dr. Watson appears in "The Adventure of the Blanched Soldier" when the detective describes his friend. "One to whom each development comes as a perpetual surprise, and to whom the future is always a closed book, is indeed an ideal helpmate."[2]

Where Holmes brought impressive skills of intelligence and deduction to the stories, Watson added heart and soul. It has been said that Watson served as the bridge between the reader and the detective. Watson, then, is often the one with whom readers best identify.

With that in mind, it is entirely possible that Watson was the most useful instrument at Holmes' disposal. (It is also entirely possible that Holmes would never admit it!) In all but four of the sixty stories, Watson is the first-person narrator.

Early in his writing, Conan Doyle decided to name Sherlock's sidekick *Ormond Sacker* before changing it to the less intimidating *Dr. John Watson*.

Fans of Sherlock Holmes are grateful.

Dr. Watson served an important role in the adventures of

Sherlock Holmes. He was the person to whom Holmes could share his most personal thoughts. In fact, readers know what Holmes is thinking primarily because the detective voices his opinions to his trusted friend. Today, whenever a character in a mystery acts as a sidekick or an assistant whom the lead detective can teach or vent to, this character is called a *Watson*.

The lesson for us is simple: if we want to learn more about God and godliness, we should pursue opportunities to teach and disciple.

Matthew 28 contains the most familiar verse about making disciples. We know from scripture that it is God's will that we urge people around us to worship God exclusively. This is the most important work we can do. But perhaps there is more. In learning the Bible so well that we can teach it to someone else, we inadvertently internalize the Word of God even better.

Second Timothy 3:16 is another familiar verse: "All Scripture is breathed out by God and profitable for teaching, for reproof, for correction, and for training in righteousness" (ESV).

Obeying the command to teach and disciple looks different for every believer. Some of us will teach Sunday school to a room of rambunctious children. Others of us will mentor teens or disciple single moms who can then turn around and disciple a family at home. Still others will stand in the pulpit and share carefully studied theological insights into the mysteries of God.

Every form of discipleship is of utmost importance to the body of Christ.

No matter what discipleship looks like for each of us, the instruction is straightforward: go into the world and make disciples.

The key to discipleship is not merely teaching someone something about God—though this is an important task. The goal is teaching someone who will teach someone else who will then teach someone else. Disciples are more than mere learners. They are multipliers. Christ set the example when He washed the disciples' feet.

> *"You call me Teacher and Lord, and you are right,*
> *for so I am. If I then, your Lord and Teacher, have*
> *washed your feet, you also ought to wash one another's*
> *feet. For I have given you an example, that you also*
> *should do just as I have done to you."*
> JOHN 13:13–15 ESV

If we belong to God, we have the tremendous privilege of internalizing God's truth by teaching it to someone else.

> *But you are a chosen race, a royal priesthood, a holy nation, a people*
> *for his own possession, that you may proclaim the excellencies of*
> *him who called you out of darkness into his marvelous light.*
> 1 PETER 2:9 ESV

16.

THICKER THAN BLOOD

"Among your many talents dissimulation finds no place."
THE ADVENTURE OF THE DYING DETECTIVE

Holmes and Watson act more like a pair of brothers than they do a set of professionals.

Thick as thieves, they still manage to criticize and pick at each other without mercy. They are quick to point out each other's shortfalls, and yet they defend each other against the world without apology.

At the end of "The Final Problem," in which Holmes plunges over Reichenbach Falls, Watson refers to Holmes as "the best and the wisest man whom I have ever known."[1] In fact, it was Arthur Conan Doyle's original plan for these words to be the last he ever wrote about the great detective.

Fortunately for those who love Sherlock Holmes, Doyle's plan did not succeed.

This tiny insight—that Watson considered Holmes to be the best and wisest man he had ever met—says volumes more about the pair than the dozens of chapters in which they bickered and squabbled.

Christopher Morley, an enthusiastic supporter of Sherlock Holmes and one of the founders of the Baker Street

Irregulars in 1934, wrote of "the wave of dismay that went around the English-reading world when Sherlock and Professor Moriarty supposedly perished together in the Reichenbach Fall."[2] If Holmes and Watson had been real-life detectives instead of brilliant imaginary heroes, no one would have felt this "wave of dismay" over Holmes' death more acutely than Dr. Watson.

For all of the pair's arguments and differences, they were true friends. They rebuked each other, and they loved each other fiercely.

Friendships like the one that belonged to Holmes and Watson are hard to come by, but it should be the aim of Christian brothers and sisters to build strong bonds in the body of Christ.

> *Two are better than one, because they have a*
> *good reward for their toil. For if they fall, one will*
> *lift up his fellow. But woe to him who is alone*
> *when he falls and has not another to lift him up!*
> ECCLESIASTES 4:9–10 ESV

We live in an age where friendships have become alliances without depth. We may interact in the halls at church or chat over social media, but too often this is the extent of our investment. Rarely do we understand the daily struggles, temptations, failures, and victories of those we consider our companions. Our relationships have been reduced to text messages and tweets.

This cannot be what God had in mind when He instructed believers to bear each other's burdens.

People talk about doing life together, but what does that really mean?

Proverbs talks about the man of many companions who comes to ruin. Perhaps one reason a man could have many friendships and still pursue sin to the point of his own destruction is because his relationships fail to go knee-deep into the struggles and celebrations of the Christian life.

Instead of viewing Christian friendships as a bonus or a hobby—something to be collected and traded like baseball cards—we must view them as a vital component of life on earth, meant to aid us on our journey to life eternal. When our schedules fill up, friendships cannot become an unnecessary expenditure, nor should we ax them from our budget of time.

For Christian friendship to be beneficial, the right kind of relationship must weather storms. The difference between believing friends and nonbelieving friends is that Christians should aim to rebuke in love and build each other up to deeds that honor God. It is the kindness of God that gives us friendships here on earth that model the long-term fellowship we will experience in heaven.

And let us consider how to stir up one another to love and good works, not neglecting to meet together, as is the habit of some, but encouraging one another, and all the more as you see the Day drawing near.
Hebrews 10:24–25 esv

Maintaining relationships that withstand trouble doesn't mean we are incapable of hurting each other or that, when we do hurt each other, we shouldn't take the proper strides to make it right. The Bible says plenty about how to treat other people in love. *Weathering storms* simply means that a friendship that falls apart at the first sign of trouble probably isn't a friendship that is designed to last.

In one of the sweetest illustrations of Christian friendship ever recorded, the Bible says, "The soul of Jonathan was knit to the soul of David, and Jonathan loved him as his own soul" (1 Samuel 18:1 esv).

We need Christian friendships. We need brothers and sisters in the body who lovingly rebuke us and who genuinely encourage us in our walk. Overlooking the resource of Christian friendship is foolish and destructive. Doing the Christian life alone only contributes to the uphill climb.

Though Holmes' and Watson's picking at each other was fictional fun and nothing more, we should consider legitimate rebuke in our relationships to be of value to us.

He who walks with wise men will be wise,
but the companion of fools will suffer harm.
Proverbs 13:20 nasb

17

MOTHER KNOWS BEST

"There is nothing new under the sun.
It has all been done before."
A STUDY IN SCARLET

One little-known fact about Arthur Conan Doyle is that he had an impressive career apart from Sherlock Holmes. Doyle was knighted by King Edward VII in 1902 for penning a pamphlet regarding the Boer War. He also wrote about World War I, in which he lost his son, brother, and two nephews. Twice, Conan Doyle ran unsuccessfully for parliament.

In addition to writing sixty adventures involving the great detective, Doyle wrote thirty-five novels and fiction collections spanning several different genres. Specifically, he had hoped that his historical romances, and not his Sherlock Holmes adventures, would define his career.

Unfortunately, when given the choice between *Micah Clarke* and *Sherlock Holmes*, most readers today only recognize the latter.

Doyle had exciting literary aspirations and eventually came to the conclusion that his Sherlock Holmes adventures were getting in the way of more important projects.

Easy solution: kill Sherlock Holmes.

When Conan Doyle decided to stop writing about Sherlock Holmes in order to put his writing career back on track, he wrote to his mother in November 1891 to explain his decision to kill off the great detective. "He takes my mind from better things," Doyle wrote. To which his mother replied, "You won't! You can't! You mustn't!"[1]

Mary Doyle was the only active parent in Conan Doyle's life since his father, Charles, was an alcoholic with a myriad of health problems. Among other unique parenting decisions, Mary required Conan Doyle to memorize and recite the family genealogy ancestor by ancestor.

Can you hear a young Conan Doyle slogging through the family tree?

In spite of this—or perhaps because of it—Conan Doyle didn't listen to his mother's advice to keep Sherlock Holmes alive. Instead, he published "The Final Problem" with no inkling how his readers would react.

In a violent struggle with his greatest nemesis, Sherlock Holmes engaged in mortal combat and plunged to an *unfortunate-albeit-convenient-for-Doyle* death over Reichenbach Falls along with Professor Moriarty. With one sentence, the British public and scads of adoring fans were thrown into mayhem:

Any attempt at recovering the bodies was absolutely
hopeless, and there, deep down in that dreadful cauldron
of swirling water and seething foam, will lie for all

time the most dangerous criminal and the foremost
champion of the law of their generation.[2]

People mourned the literary death of Sherlock Holmes as if a real-life public figure had died. A historic marker has been erected at Reichenbach Falls that reads, "In this fearful place Sherlock Holmes vanquished Professor Moriarty on May 1891."

No one was more surprised by the public response than Doyle, who still had no idea that Sherlock Holmes would be his writing legacy. Doyle had no choice but to resurrect his dead detective, which he did in *The Return of Sherlock Holmes.*

Not surprising: Mom was right.

And though Conan Doyle had no biblical mandate to keep the great detective alive, he would have been wise to listen to the advice of those who most wanted him to succeed.

Perhaps the greatest lesson in this story is to seek and listen to the counsel of those who know and love us best. God never intended us to *go it alone* in the Christian life. One of the great deceptions we buy into is self-sovereignty. We think we know best how to live our lives. Sometimes we even believe we know better than our Creator.

God designed us to be dependent creatures. From the creation of the first man, God intended humans to be social beings. What did God say in Genesis 2:18? "It is not good that the man should be alone; I will make him a helper fit for him" (ESV).

Proverbs 11:14 it says: "Where there is no guidance, a people falls, but in an abundance of counselors there is safety" (11:14).

We must utilize the invaluable resource God has placed in our lives in the form of Christian counselors. These family members, church members, or close friends ought to comprise our circle of advisors whom we turn to for prayer and guidance.

Getting counsel from godly people is a directive from God for our own protection. Certainly an entire group of imperfect people can come to an imperfect decision, but the chances are small by comparison to one person making important decisions alone. Not availing ourselves of counsel is setting ourselves up for voluntary failure. Where self-sufficiency says, "I don't need you!" accountability cries, "Help!" and reaps the benefits of a life in Christian community.

God often uses events and struggles in our lives to remind us that we can do nothing apart from Him. One means of His grace and assistance is providing us with a multitude of counselors who can pray with and for us about the needs of our lives.

Had Conan Doyle listened to his mother, he might have saved Sherlock Holmes from an unnecessarily dramatic reappearance.

There is no new thing under the sun.
ECCLESIASTES 1:9 KJV

18.

PLAYING FAVORITES

"The work is its own reward."

THE ADVENTURE OF THE NORWOOD BUILDER

Arthur Conan Doyle was asked to list his favorite Sherlock Holmes stories. With sixty to choose from, this could not have been an easy task, but he eventually completed the assignment. His first five favorites in order are as follows:

1. "The Adventure of the Speckled Band"
2. "The Adventure of the Red-Headed League"
3. "The Adventure of the Dancing Men"
4. "The Final Problem"
5. "A Scandal in Bohemia"

For a full listing, see pages 302–304. Any reader new to Sherlock Holmes should consider beginning with this list.

It is no surprise that Conan Doyle picked "The Adventure of the Speckled Band" as his ultimate favorite. The story has all the markings of a fantastic read—a damsel in distress, a strange death, and a heartless stepfather named Grimesby Roylott. (Arthur Conan Doyle was a master at creating unique names for his characters.)

"The Adventure of the Speckled Band" has been easily and often adapted for stage, radio, and television audiences. It is considered one of four *locked-room mysteries* in the canon. A locked-room mystery is a detective story in which a crime is committed under seemingly impossible circumstances. For instance, a murder is committed in a room where no one has the ability to enter or leave (thus the name *locked room*). The story usually presents all the clues and evidence, and then it nudges the reader to solve the mystery before the case is dramatically explained in a final scene or chapter.

Despite the immense success of Sherlock Holmes, Conan Doyle never loved the great detective as much as his loyal readers did. Even after bringing Holmes back from his dramatic almost-death over Reichenbach Falls, Doyle seemed to resent the detective, who had become larger than life.

The reason? Sherlock Holmes' fame eclipsed that of Conan Doyle, leading readers to theorize that Doyle resented the character he had created. How often has Sherlock Holmes been credited for introducing forensic science and improving criminal profiling? How often is the great detective recognized for his scientific experiments and brilliant deductive reasoning? Sherlock Holmes is given incredible accolades and honors for his accomplishments. And yet, in reality, every achievement belongs to Conan Doyle.

An actor wrote to Conan Doyle and asked permission to

use creative license to allow Sherlock Holmes to get married in an upcoming play. As the story is told, Doyle responded: "You may marry him or murder him or do whatever you like with him".

The author did not love his work where Sherlock Holmes was concerned.

In "The Norwood Builder," a reclusive bachelor disappears from his home the night before a massive fire on his property. The bachelor's bed is ruffled, his safe is cracked, his papers are scattered, and signs of trouble exist all around. The suspect goes to Sherlock Holmes and asks for help, and Holmes solves the crime. In the pages of the story, Holmes allows one of the inspectors to take credit for solving the crime and the following conversation ensues:

> *"And you don't want your name to appear?" [asks Inspector Lestrade.]*
>
> *"Not at all. The work is its own reward. Perhaps I shall get the credit also at some distant day when I permit my zealous historian to lay out his foolscap once more—eh, Watson?"*[1]

Sherlock Holmes loved his work, while Conan Doyle did not.

Doyle might have agreed with Mark Twain, a contemporary, when he said, "Work is a necessary evil to be avoided."[2]

As Christians, we should do everything in our power

not to view our work with angst or resentment. We have the unique opportunity to honor God in whatever work He has called us to do. When we rely on God to manifest His power in us so that we can accomplish excellent work, it doesn't matter what job we are called to do, we glorify Him. "So, whether you eat or drink, or whatever you do, do all to the glory of God" (1 Corinthians 10:31 ESV).

As believers in the work place, we can exalt God in many ways. Being honest, encouraging others, working hard, and showing kindness can set us apart from the majority of the work force almost immediately. The key? We must learn to work for God in spite of a fickle boss or unpredictable co-worker. We must make God's expectations of us our chief concern.

Not by the way of eye-service, as people-pleasers, but as bondservants of Christ, doing the will of God from the heart, rendering service with a good will as to the Lord and not to man.
EPHESIANS 6:6–7 ESV

Arthur Conan Doyle may have disliked Sherlock Holmes because the detective was getting in the way of better ideas and bigger dreams. Though we may not experience an imaginary character overshadowing our personal success in this life, we can identify with frustration over current work getting in the way of bigger ambitions. Unending school days, entry-level jobs, or difficult managers can become our Sherlock Holmes. We can feel overlooked, undervalued, or unappreciated. How many of us have watched ambitious coworkers or fellow classmates take credit for work we accomplished?

We must keep in mind that God has called us to our current task and will give us the necessary strength to accomplish our responsibilities for His glory. We must become convinced that all work—if it is honorable—has the equal opportunity to be holy if it is done for God. We fulfill our purpose by obeying God and reflecting His character.

No doubt Jesus the carpenter was able to glorify God long before He went to the cross.

And people should eat and drink and enjoy the fruits of their labor, for these are gifts from God.
ECCLESIASTES 3:13 NLT

19.

BY MISTAKE

"So silent and furtive were his movements, like those of a trained bloodhound picking out a scent, that I could not but think what a terrible criminal he would have made had he turned his energy and sagacity against the law instead of exerting them in its defense."
THE SIGN OF FOUR

Sherlock enthusiasts love nothing more than a good contradiction.

Arthur Conan Doyle wrote fifty-six short stories and four novels featuring the great detective, and he wrote most of these very quickly. Twenty-seven-year-old Conan Doyle wrote his debut Sherlock Holmes novel, *A Study in Scarlet*, in just three weeks. Without the modern conveniences of a computer or Internet search engine, keeping track of the enormous number of details surrounding the complicated characters was nearly unmanageable.

If that didn't provide enough of a challenge, Conan Doyle did not write his stories in order of when they happened to the detective. He wrote all over the timeline of Sherlock Holmes' life.

Sometimes Conan Doyle noted the time frame in a story,

and sometimes he merely alluded to historical events that enabled readers to place the date; but either way, the stories were not written chronologically. One story about the detective might precede a story that happened earlier in Holmes' career and vice versa. Because of this disjointed time line and the lack of a search feature that could quickly scan his documents for discrepancies, Doyle sometimes forgot that he had already introduced a pair of characters or mentioned the details of a specific event. Sherlockians love to cross-reference these stories and point to impossibilities. They search for errors the way children hunt for eggs on Easter morning.

As the collection of Holmes' adventures grew, so, too, did the number of inaccuracies. And where this might infuriate literary enthusiasts, instead reconciling the differences is a favorite pastime for Holmes' devotees. Serious fans of Sherlock Holmes have studied weather reports, scoured almanacs, interviewed historians, and have constructed detailed chronologies of the criminal cases in the canon. And whenever they have stumbled on an incorrect date or historical impossibility, they have attributed the oversight to Dr. Watson, who was obviously careless about his records.

Poor Dr. Watson!

To the degree that Sherlock Holmes is given credit for Conan Doyle's successes, Dr. Watson is blamed for Conan Doyle's mistakes.

One of the more humorous inconsistencies in the canon is the fact that Dr. Watson can't seem to remember the date of his own marriage. This doesn't bode well for the number of wives some Sherlockians have tried to attribute to the kind doctor.

Another well-known discrepancy involves the injury Dr. Watson received during the Battle of Maiwand. *A Study in Scarlet* describes the wound as being a bullet to the shoulder, but by the time we read *The Sign of Four*, the injury has shifted to his leg. Later, in "The Adventure of the Noble Bachelor," Watson is again speaking of his injury when he says: "And the Jezail bullet which I had brought back in one of my limbs as a relic of my Afghan campaign throbbed with dull persistence."[1]

You can almost see a frustrated Conan Doyle throwing his hands in the air while trying to remember where his beloved Dr. Watson had been injured. And arriving to no confident conclusion, he writes "in one of my limbs" so as to cover all the bases.

All things considered, the canon is an impressive literary accomplishment. The inconsistencies simply point to the fact that the stories and novels are a work of fiction. Conan Doyle didn't have witnesses or historical documents at his disposal. He had only his rich imagination to work with.

The Bible is not fiction.

Studying the works of Sherlock Holmes—replete with

contradictions and impossibilities—only makes the Bible that much more extraordinary because every word is consistent and true.

God's Word is broader in scope and deeper in implication than Conan Doyle's canon, and yet it remains an infallible authority because it is God's inspired Word. In other words, the Bible is true and trustworthy because God is true and trustworthy.

If we are impressed that an imperfect man, Arthur Conan Doyle, could write sixty imperfect stories about a fictional detective, we should be infinitely more impressed that God used forty different imperfect authors speaking three different languages from three separate continents over two thousand years to pen the words of scripture. And every word in the Bible is trustworthy.

How is this possible? "For no prophecy was ever produced by the will of man, but men spoke from God as they were carried along by the Holy Spirit" (2 Peter 1:21 esv). No book in the world is a match for the Bible. God's Word is inspired and inerrant. It stands on its own authority. We ought to say with the weeping prophet: "Your words were found, and I ate them, and your words became to me a joy and the delight of my heart, for I am called by your name, O Lord, God of hosts" (Jeremiah 15:16 esv).

To keep God's Word, we've got to internalize it. To internalize it, we need to read it.

Every word of God proves true; he is a shield to those who take refuge in him. Do not add to his words, lest he rebuke you and you be found a liar.

PROVERBS 30:5–6 ESV

20

MATRON OF HONOR

"Life is infinitely stranger than anything
which the mind of man could invent."
A CASE OF IDENTITY

There is no telling if Conan Doyle intended for Mrs. Hudson—the landlady at 221B Baker Street—to become such a well-known and much-loved figure in the adventures of Sherlock Holmes. But that is exactly what happened.

Though we are never given a first name or physical description of this landlady, she is a reliable presence in the stories nonetheless. Mrs. Hudson became a sort of gatekeeper to 221B Baker Street as hordes of guests and clients crossed the threshold and climbed the seventeen uncarpeted and rather shoddy stairs to consult with the great detective. Over time, she became a vital member of the three-person team that included Holmes and Watson.

Mrs. Hudson, by necessity, was a long-suffering woman. The opening lines of "The Adventure of the Dying Detective" include a list of Holmes' weaknesses, including his:

Incredible untidiness, his addiction to music at strange
hours, his occasional revolver practice within doors,

his weird and often malodorous scientific experiments,
and the atmosphere of violence and danger which
hung around him made him the very worst tenant in
London.[1]

Perhaps, though there is no scientific evidence to support this theory, Sherlock Holmes is the reason landlords now require deposits from new tenants.

Still, for whatever reasons, Mrs. Hudson maintained the deepest awe for the detective, never interfering with his work or requesting he take his strange employment elsewhere. She may have been the only person in the canon who believed— and likewise said—that Holmes was gentle and courteous to women. Maybe this belief indicates, more than anything, that Holmes had a soft spot in his heart for the housekeeper and was uncharacteristically kind to her.

Mrs. Hudson lived a simple life, yet she chose to enjoy the adventures that came with assisting Holmes and Watson. For the most part, she liked meeting the clients that came to see the detective, and she enjoyed caring for Holmes and Watson whenever they let her. She never complained about the endless hours Holmes conducted business or about the type of people he paraded across the threshold of her home.

Simply put, Mrs. Hudson loved living.

As Christians, we should take seriously the pursuit of our joy. Sometimes we get caught up in following rules and obeying obligations—all necessary components to living thoughtful, submissive lives—but our Christian walk can easily become discipline without delight.

How often in literature or life has the Christian character been portrayed as the stuffy busybody whose chief objective is to push morals and judge shortcomings—a sort of Rachel Lynde in the world of *Anne of Green Gables*?

This is not God's design. God desires that we say with the psalmist:

> *I have set the LORD always before me; because he is at my*
> *right hand, I shall not be shaken. Therefore my heart is glad,*
> *and my whole being rejoices; my flesh also dwells secure.*
> PSALM 16:8–9 ESV

Joy should be a trademark of the Christian faith.

God wants us to delight in Him. Furthermore, He wants us to delight in living. First Timothy tells us that God richly provides us with everything to enjoy. In other words, we have no excuse not to pursue joy in our temporary existence on this planet. The best is yet to come!

Unfortunately, it is easy to complicate the concept. We buy into the lie that a promotion at work or the acknowledgement of a peer or the accomplishment of a goal will bring us the happiness that we crave. In reality, everything we need to be joyful is found in Jesus Christ.

One of the overlooked motivations that prompted Christ to go to the cross is found in Hebrews.

> *Looking to Jesus, the founder and perfecter of our faith, who for the joy that was set before him endured the cross, despising the shame, and is seated at the right hand of the throne of God.*
> HEBREWS 12:2 ESV

Christ endured the cross *for the joy that was set before Him.*

His joy should motivate our own. If Jesus could go to the cross for the joy that was set before Him, certainly we can endure any struggles or disappointments in this life for the joy that is set before us.

Look around. God has given us amazing opportunities. The fact that we woke up this morning is a gift that wasn't afforded to everyone. Furthermore, God promises to meet every one of our needs—something not promised to the unbeliever. So we can assume that anything we lack is unnecessary to the fulfillment of our joy.

We should pray for ourselves and for each other these words—"May the God of hope fill you with all joy and peace in believing, so that by the power of the Holy Spirit you may abound in hope" (Romans 15:13 ESV).

May we be a Mrs. Hudson—simple, joyful stewards of the tasks before us. One thing that may have contributed to the housekeeper's happiness is the fact that she understood her role. She did not sign up for Holmes and Watson to serve her—she committed to serve them.

This simple shift in thinking—preferring to serve instead of be served—makes a world of difference.

For as the heavens are higher than the earth, so are my ways higher than your ways and my thoughts than your thoughts.
ISAIAH 55:9 ESV

21.

THE PRINCE OF CRIME

"It is fortunate for this community
that I am not a criminal."

THE ADVENTURE OF THE BRUCE-PARTINGTON PLANS

When Arthur Conan Doyle began writing about Sherlock Holmes, crime fiction didn't exist. He drew on inspiration from favorite writers, newspaper stories, and local advertisements. He gave a published nod to one of his biggest influences in the second chapter of his first detective novel, *A Study in Scarlet*. Dr. Watson, speaking to Sherlock Holmes, says: "'It is simple enough as you explain it,' I said, smiling. 'You remind me of Edgar Allan Poe's Dupin. I had no idea that such individuals did exist outside of stories.'"[1] Using Sherlock Holmes to reference Auguste Dupin is a reader's *dream within a dream*.

How did Sherlock Holmes respond to the comparison to Dupin, believed to be the very first fictional detective?

Sherlock Holmes rose and lit his pipe. "No doubt you think that you are complimenting me in comparing me to Dupin," he observed. "Now, in my opinion, Dupin was a very inferior fellow. That trick of his of breaking in on his friends' thoughts with an apropos remark after a quarter of an hour's silence is really very showy and superficial. He had some analytical genius, no doubt; but he was by no means such a phenomenon as Poe appeared to imagine."[2]

According to legend, a loyal reader of Edgar Allan Poe wrote Conan Doyle a scathing letter for criticizing Dupin. Doyle's response? "I didn't do it. Holmes did!"[3]

Well played, Conan Doyle.

In "The Adventure of the Bruce-Partington Plans," a dense yellow fog has settled down upon London, and Watson is scouring the newspaper looking for interesting criminal activity to report to Holmes. "There was the news of a revolution, of a possible war, and of an impending change of government."[4]

Interesting, isn't it, that our newspapers today contain the same topics?

None of this news interested the mastermind detective.

Greasy brown swirls drift past the window at 221B Baker Street, leaving oily drops on the windowpanes, and Holmes says to his companion: "This great and somber stage is set for something more worthy than that. It is fortunate for this community that I am not a criminal."[5] Without realizing it, Sherlock Holmes spoke spiritual truth with these words.

If we could understand the extent of the deceitfulness of

our own hearts, we would likely agree with Sherlock Holmes—
It is fortunate for this community that I am not a criminal.

> *As it is written: "None is righteous, no, not one; no one
> understands; no one seeks for God. All have turned aside;
> together they have become worthless; no one does good,
> not even one. Their throat is an open grave; they use
> their tongues to deceive. The venom of asps is under their
> lips. Their mouth is full of curses and bitterness."*
> ROMANS 3:10–14 ESV

Popular psychology likes to assume that our hearts are the
best part about us. We commonly hear phrases like "Follow
your heart" or "Trust your heart," and these instructions
assume the heart could never lead us astray. When was the
last time you heard someone caution an individual about listening to her heart? Watch an afternoon of television talk
shows and you will be hard pressed to find a host who
cautions a guest against doing what his heart tells him to
do, no matter how foolish the desire or decision may appear
to be.

This concept runs contrary to all we know to be true
from scripture. In fact, God came to save us from our hearts,
which are desperately wicked. Our heart is fundamentally
flawed and out of line if God and His good purposes are not
central to it. Better to say, "Follow God!" or even better, "Trust

in the LORD with all your heart, and lean not on your own understanding" (Proverbs 3:5 NKJV).

In learning the power of our hearts, it is essential that we understand the problems we face are not primarily outside of us but inside of us. Our hearts—as opposed to our circumstances—are the primary problem when we are caught in sin. Thus God came to change our hearts and not necessarily our troubles.

> *"For from within, out of the heart of man,*
> *come evil thoughts, sexual immorality, theft, murder,*
> *adultery, coveting, wickedness, deceit, sensuality,*
> *envy, slander, pride, foolishness. All these evil things*
> *come from within, and they defile a person."*
> MARK 7:21–23 ESV

The good news is that though our hearts are naturally evil, God doesn't leave them that way when He adopts us into His family. He gives us wisdom to overcome our feelings, He gives us discernment to distinguish feelings from reality, and He gives us the grace to reject feelings that run contrary to the truth of God.

When 2 Corinthians 5:17 says, "Therefore if anyone is in Christ, he is a new creature; the old things passed away; behold, new things have come" (NASB), we understand it to mean that Christ took the would-be criminal and made him a child of God. This radical change is not the result of following our heart, but of following God. It is not the consequence of trusting ourselves, but of trusting our Savior.

At the heart of every problem is a problem of the heart. Indeed, it is fortunate for our communities that we are not criminals.

> *The heart is deceitful above all things,*
> *and desperately sick; who can understand it?*
> JEREMIAH 17:9 ESV

22.

JUSTICE FOR HIRE

"It's every man's business to see justice done."
THE ADVENTURE OF THE CROOKED MAN

Sherlock Holmes was willing to do whatever it took to win a case.

Take, for instance, "The Adventure of Charles Augustus Milverton." Holmes is hired by the debutante Lady Eva Blackwell, whom Holmes calls "the most beautiful debutante of last season," to retrieve some compromising letters that have fallen into the hands of a blackmailer named Milverton. Basically, Milverton is attempting to extort Blackwell before her marriage, and the nervous bride-to-be is willing to do whatever it takes to stop him. And, raising the stakes even higher, Milverton is the king of blackmailers—called "the worst man in London."

So the stage is set: the greatest detective is pitted against the greatest blackmailer in a race to save or destroy the most beautiful debutante.

Who will emerge the victor?

Milverton demands seven thousand pounds (or roughly twelve thousand dollars) from Lady Eva Blackwell. The year is 1899, so losing this sum of money to the blackmailer would certainly destroy Blackwell, ending her current marriage engagement and reducing her reputation to ash. Everything she has is on the line.

Sherlock Holmes exists for cases like this one.

And because we know from his treatment of the king in "A Scandal in Bohemia" that Holmes hates the upper class, we can be confident that he wants to rescue Lady Eva Blackwell less because of a benevolent heart and more because of a desire to win.

Holmes loves nothing more than being right.

In typical Holmes style, he disguises himself as a plumber and visits Milverton's Hampstead house in order to assess the home's layout and observe his rival's daily routine. The detective needs to know where Milverton hides his most important papers, and specifically where he is keeping the compromising letters.

In order to secure his safety in the house, Holmes befriends Milverton's housemaid, going so far as to propose marriage to her. The conversation between Holmes and Watson goes as follows:

> *"You would not call me a marrying man, Watson?"*
> *"No, indeed!"*
> *"You'll be interested to hear that I'm engaged."*
> *"My dear fellow! I congrat—"*
> *"To Milverton's housemaid."*

"Good heavens, Holmes!"
"I wanted information, Watson."
"Surely you have gone too far?"
It was a most necessary step."[1]

Holmes solves the crime, of course, and saves Eva Blackwell from poverty and shame. It should also be noted, however, that Holmes walked away from the housemaid without so much as a backward glance. Readers are not given any indication that Holmes spoke to or explained himself to the girl to whom he pledged marriage. Unfortunately, this type of behavior was not unique to Holmes. His goal was to solve crimes at any cost.

Who emerged the winner? No one.

Justice is important. Even our nonreligious culture places a tremendous emphasis on justice. Perhaps nothing fires us up the way injustice does—the kidnapping of hundreds of little girls overseas or the beating of a pregnant Christian woman in a country that devalues Jesus Christ. Smaller injustices also beg our attention. School bullying or workplace discrimination can be devastating.

Looking at the totality of God's Word, it is difficult to make a case that justice doesn't matter. Of course it does. But the requirements of the Christian life do not end with getting what's right or even trampling what's wrong. Micah 6:8 contains God's blueprint for living: "He has told you, O man, what is good; and what does the LORD require of you but to do justice, and to love kindness, and to walk humbly with your God?" (ESV)

Walking humbly with God is learning to walk in step with Him and value what He most values. And what is that? Doing justice and loving mercy. At first glance, these commands seem like separate items on a spiritual to-do list, but in reality they are one and the same. Because of how the sentence was arranged in the original language, it would be correct to understand it as: *We must walk with God and do justice out of mercy.*

If and when we achieve justice at the expense of hurting other people—even people we believe to be wrong—we have missed the point. Holding hateful signs or spouting harmful words laced with biblical truth is never God's desire.

The great detective was good at solving crime—no doubt about it—but he did it for himself and not for the good of other people. Otherwise, he wouldn't have left a housemaid in the dust.

As believers, we must be more than simply justice for hire.

> *To do righteousness and justice is more*
> *acceptable to the LORD than sacrifice.*
> PROVERBS 21:3 ESV

23.

FULCRUM FILES

*"Good old Watson! You are the
one fixed point in a changing age."*
HIS LAST BOW

Throughout Conan Doyle's sixty stories featuring Sherlock Holmes, people and settings frequently change. Doyle introduces more than three hundred characters during Holmes' career. Every story is a world unto itself. And yet, in spite of all this change, a few people and places remain the same. In the words of Holmes, they are a "fixed point in a changing age."[1]

One of those fixed points is 221B Baker Street—perhaps the most famous bachelor pad in the history of literature and one of the most consistent elements in the stories featuring Sherlock Holmes.

The most familiar setting in the canon is the simple but comfortable residence where Holmes—and Dr. Watson when he wasn't married—lived over the course of twenty years. Nearly every one of Conan Doyle's stories about Holmes began or ended at 221B Baker Street. This address became such an iconic part of the adventures of Sherlock Holmes that the Abbey National Building Society in London had to hire a full-time secretary to handle all of the mail that came to this actual address.

According to *A Study in Scarlet*: "221B Baker Street consisted of a couple of comfortable bed-rooms and a single large airy sitting-room, cheerfully furnished, and illuminated by two broad windows."[2] The living space was much less impressive than the work and friendship that happened within its walls, but it served as a necessary backdrop to the great detective's many adventures.

Baker Street's 221B has been called the world's most famous address. A Sherlock Holmes Museum on London's Baker Street has recreated the great detective's rooms down to the tiniest detail, meaning 221B Baker Street *still* exists today. In exchange for a few dollars, eager tourists can climb the seventeen stairs where Mrs. Hudson led anxious clients to the waiting detective. Sightseers can then catch a glimpse of the acid-stained table where Holmes did his toughest experiments or view the chair where Holmes employed his best thinking at the beginning of a complex case.

Thankfully, it would stand to reason that the room is less smoky now than it was when Conan Doyle's character inhabited it.

Interested readers who cannot travel to the home of the mastermind detective should send a letter to 221B Baker Street, London NW1 6XE, England. Some recipients have been known to receive a leather bookmark or set of commemorative stamps in response. The secretary to Sherlock

Holmes responds to hundreds of letters each year, kindly responding with something along these lines: "When Mr. Holmes was last heard from, he had retired to Sussex to keep bees."

For fans of Sherlock Holmes, 221B Baker Street is and always has been a fixed point. For the believer, God is our fixed point in a changing age.

Thousands of things may change for us during the course of a lifetime. Our address may change or the number of members in our family may shift. Our relationships with friends may improve or decline. We may experience seasons of overwhelming happiness or periods of deep grief. Everything we hold dear can be swept away in a space of a moment.

But God never changes.

Albert Simpson, a Canadian preacher and contemporary of Arthur Conan Doyle, penned the song:

Yesterday, today, forever, Jesus is the same.
All may change, but Jesus never! Glory to His name![3]

The song is simple but profound.

Though we may be tempted to change our minds or moods one hundred times in a single afternoon, God never changes. His choices are not governed by feelings or fears, but are driven by the holiness of His inflexible character. So that what He says in His Word, He means. "God is not man, that he should lie, or a son of man, that he should change his mind. Has he said, and will he not do it? Or has he spoken, and will he not fulfill it?" (Numbers 23:19 ESV).

The fact that God is the same yesterday, today, and forever cuts against the grain of progressive thinking. As a culture, we prize the *new*, the *innovative*, and the *improved*. When was the last time you heard someone boast that he owned the oldest cell phone in the room or she still wore the same shoes she wore a decade ago?

God needs no improvement and neither does the truth in His Word. Yesterday God directed your steps with absolute authority. Today He will grant you the wisdom you need to make every decision. Tomorrow He will guide you with His almighty hand.

The changelessness of God should inspire us to trust Him with the entirety of our lives. We should be so filled with profound contentment that, in a world that constantly changes, we can say with the hymnist, Edward Mote:

> *When darkness veils His lovely face,*
> *I rest on His unchanging grace;*
> *In every high and stormy gale,*
> *My anchor holds within the veil.*
> *On Christ, the solid Rock, I stand;*
> *All other ground is sinking sand.*[4]

Our baseline for stability in this life must be God alone. He is our fixed point in a changing age.

> *"I the LORD do not change."*
> MALACHI 3:6 NIV

24.

ON PURPOSE

*"My life is spent in one long effort to
escape from the commonplaces of existence.
These little problems help me to do so."*
THE ADVENTURE OF THE RED-HEADED LEAGUE

Sherlock Holmes lived to solve crimes.

More specifically, Holmes lived to prove he was right. He loved nothing more than the magical moment when he could stand in a room of slack-jawed observers and explain how he traveled from the tiniest bit of evidence to the grandest sentences of guilt. These occasions never failed to impress.

Because crime solving was his passion, Holmes didn't complain when his apartment was overrun late at night by characters from the wrong part of town requesting his assistance. He didn't bemoan his lack of privacy or his over-abundance of requests. He played his violin, he shot his revolver, he smoked his pipe—he did whatever helped him accomplish one goal: Holmes wanted to solve mysteries—the tougher the challenge, the greater the appeal.

And yet, in the final paragraphs of "The Red-Headed League"—arguably one of the most difficult cases Holmes was asked to investigate in the canon—he says: "My life is spent in one long effort to escape from the commonplaces of existence. These little problems help me to do so."[1] So on one hand Holmes lived to do what he loved, and on the other hand, he found much of his life to be a monotonous existence. How sad to enjoy what you do and yet still find life tedious. How is that possible?

Life is futile if we live for what will decay.

In His Word, God continually calls us to look at things eternally—that is, to see things from His perspective. This is the great challenge of the Christian life.

> *If then you have been raised with Christ,*
> *seek the things that are above, where Christ is,*
> *seated at the right hand of God. Set your minds on*
> *things that are above, not on things that are on earth.*
> COLOSSIANS 3:1–2 ESV

It has been said that prosperity—not poverty—is the worst trial many of us will face in this life. This prosperity doesn't necessarily include a gargantuan amount of money or an impressive number of toys. Any *thing* that gives us security and leads us to believe we do not need God, which in turn leads us to conclusions that permanently separate us from Him, is the worst type of trial in this life.

Remember: things will never satisfy the human heart.

From the first story in the Bible and in every one thereafter, man has struggled to place less value on God's creation than on God Himself. Satan understands this to be true of the human heart. In the first chapter of Job where Satan is making a case about God's servant, Satan asks the Lord:

"Does Job fear God for no reason? Have you not put
a hedge around him and his house and all that he has,
on every side? You have blessed the work of his hands,
and his possessions have increased in the land. But
stretch out your hand and touch all that he has,
and he will curse you to your face."
JOB 1:9–11 ESV

Satan confidently believed if God would take Job's *stuff* away, then Job would curse God—a sad indictment on the human heart. Even as the children of God, we often choose to live for what won't last. *Stuff* more than anything distracts us from eternity.

We must follow the example of Christ, who "emptied himself, by taking the form of a servant, being born in the likeness of men. And being found in human form, he humbled himself by becoming obedient to the point of death, even death on a cross" (Philippians 2:7–8 ESV).

The problem with earthly ambition and accumulation is that, eventually, it will all decay. Charles Studd was a British missionary who lived at the same time as Arthur Conan

Doyle. Studd wrote a poem that includes the words:

> *Only one life, 'twill soon be past,*
> *Only what's done for Christ will last.*
> *And when I am dying, how happy I'll be,*
> *If the lamp of my life has been burned out for Thee.*[2]

The challenge, then, is easier said than done: give yourself away for the glory of God. Burn out the lamp of your life in service to your Savior. No one when looking at the face of Jesus for the first time will wish he had done less for God.

The temptation is often to believe that we deserve a better life than the one we have been given. In reality, a better life might make it even harder to live with an eternal perspective. Any earthbound *thing* that threatens our relationship with God is not worth the effort it takes to keep it. Christ poured Himself out—giving His life away for a cause that was bigger than any material possession. He has invited us to follow His example.

We will be most generous with the people around us when we remember how generous God has been to us.

> *"Don't store up treasures here on earth, where moths eat them and rust destroys them, and where thieves break in and steal."*
> MATTHEW 6:19 NLT

25.

ALL IN A NAME

*"It has long been an axiom of mine that the
little things are infinitely the most important."*
A CASE OF IDENTITY

The name *Sherlock Holmes* lends itself easily to spoofs and spin-offs.

During the past one hundred years, dozens of parodies have yielded endless versions of Sherlock Holmes' name, including *Sherlock Bones, Doorlock Homes, Unlock Homes, Shamrock Jolnes, Sheerlock Jones*, and *Sure Luck*. These names do not even scratch the surface of the number of variations that have been created. Even Arthur Conan Doyle, by the end of his career, joined in the pastime of poking fun at the great detective.

Throughout the canon, Sherlock Holmes draws attention to the reality that the small things make the biggest difference. No doubt "the small things" include even the name of a character. Arthur Conan Doyle, known for giving his characters peculiar names, intended to name the great detective *Sherrinford Holmes*, while calling Holmes' sidekick *Ormond Sacker*. Mrs. Hudson was originally going to be named *Mrs. Turner*.

Interesting to note, Conan Doyle was certain about the last name of *Holmes*, since Oliver Wendell Holmes was a physician and poet whom Doyle greatly admired.

Details are important. More specifically, names are important.

The most significant name for God in the Old Testament also happens to be the most commonly used name for God in the Bible. The name is so important that it often appears in capital letters. The Hebrew spelling is YHWH, and it is often pronounced *Yahweh*.

The name *Yahweh* carries so much significance that observant Jews have historically refused to say the name aloud for fear they might say it without the proper amount of honor or respect. They carefully observe the command: "You shall not take the name of the LORD your God in vain, for the LORD will not hold him guiltless who takes his name in vain" (Exodus 20:7 ESV).

"Taking the name of the Lord in vain" essentially means emptying the name of its significance. Whenever Jewish people arrive at this precious name while reading the Old Testament aloud, they use a different name, *Adonai*, as an added precaution.

YHWH appears almost seven thousand times in the Old Testament. Its meaning can best be understood from a well-known story in the Old Testament:

Then Moses said to God, "If I come to the people of Israel
and say to them, 'The God of your fathers has sent me to
you,' and they ask me, 'What is his name?' what shall I
say to them?" God said to Moses, "I AM WHO I AM." And
he said, "Say this to the people of Israel, 'I AM has sent me
to you.'" God also said to Moses, "Say this to the people
of Israel, 'The LORD, the God of your fathers, the God of
Abraham, the God of Isaac, and the God of Jacob, has
sent me to you.' This is my name forever, and thus I am
to be remembered throughout all generations."
EXODUS 3:13–15 ESV

God's people treasured His name, which basically means *I
am* or *I will be what I will be.* They demonstrated that it is
impossible to love and respect the name of God too much.

No doubt their reverence for the name only reflects their
adoration for God Himself.

We live in a culture that is far removed from this type of
regard for God. Even Christian people who love their heavenly Father are comfortable telling jokes or creating comics
where God is the punch line. We confuse sacred songs and silly
tunes, and we spout euphemisms in everyday conversation. We
mindlessly fill the dead space of our praying aloud with God's
name while we think of what to say next.

In many ways, the purity of God's name has been entirely
lost in our generation.

Unfortunately, even within the stories of Sherlock Holmes, it is possible to find examples where Sir Arthur Conan Doyle took liberty with God's name. This is a sad indictment on the author's view of his Creator.

True, most of us don't spout God's name in a moment of anger or speak Christ's name in a moment of surprise, but taking God's name in vain—emptying the name of its significance—happens in a myriad of other ways. If we sing or speak the name of our heavenly Father without infusing our words with the worship He deserves, we have spoken His name in vain.

We should long to say with the psalmist: "Teach me your way, O LORD, that I may walk in your truth; unite my heart to fear your name" (Psalm 86:11 ESV).

We need to be very careful when we talk about our heavenly Father, remembering who He is and what He has done for us. Knowing and speaking God's name is an enormous privilege that was given to us at great cost.

> *"The good person out of the good treasure of his heart produces good, and the evil person out of his evil treasure produces evil, for out of the abundance of the heart his mouth speaks."*
> LUKE 6:45 ESV

26

GOOD CHEMISTRY

*"How often have I said to you that when you
have eliminated the impossible, whatever remains,
however improbable, must be the truth?"*
THE SIGN OF FOUR

Arthur Conan Doyle was not initially successful with Sherlock Holmes. When he published his first novel, *A Study in Scarlet*, Doyle was a married twenty-six-year-old general practitioner with aspirations to be a writer. When he finally decided to pen his first story about the great detective, the novel was not well received. Sherlock Holmes, after all, was years ahead of his time, solving crimes because of the mistakes of the criminal as much as the intelligence of the detective.

The title of Doyle's first novel was derived from a line in the story: "There's the scarlet thread of murder running through the colourless skein of life, and our duty is to unravel it, and isolate it, and expose every inch of it."[1] And with those words, *A Study in Scarlet* was born.

Eventually, the world caught the coattails of Conan Doyle's dream, and Sherlock Holmes found a permanent spot on the bookshelves of readers worldwide.

No one was more surprised by this sudden and certain success than Conan Doyle.

Of all the accolades Sherlock Holmes heaped on himself—and there have been many during the last century—none is quite so impressive as his posthumous Honorary Fellowship from the Royal Society of Chemistry. In 2002, Holmes became the first fictional character to receive this honor.

Historically, the award has been given to Nobel laureates, including the great Alfred Nobel himself, or other highly distinguished real people who have made an impact on education or industry. In 2002, the rules were bent in order to honor the fictional character who brought scientific logic and practice to the world of crime solving.

Essentially, Sherlock Holmes, the fictional character, has been more beneficial to science than many living scientists.

If someone had told Arthur Conan Doyle after *A Study in Scarlet* was published in the nineteenth century and failed to meet expectations that during the twenty-first century Sherlock Holmes would be invited to join a distinguished society of scientists, Doyle likely would have laughed in the face of the messenger.

Sherlock Holmes overcame his own fictional limitations when he joined the Royal Society of Chemistry. Strange? Yes, but stranger things have happened. For instance: "Then the LORD God formed a man from the dust of the ground and breathed into his nostrils the breath of life, and the man became a living being" (Genesis 2:7 NIV). Furthermore, God chose to take this dust and make it part of His family.

Our God delights in doing the impossible.

Hebrews 11 contains the record of a more impressive society—the men and women who, by faith, trusted God with the impossibilities of their lives. "Now faith is the assurance of things hoped for, the conviction of things not seen. For by it the people of old received their commendation" (Hebrews 11:1–2 ESV).

Even more impressive than any inclusion into the Royal Society of Chemistry, God ordained men and women to receive the honor that came with enduring faith. What is this enduring faith? It is more than a casual belief in God. It is even more than a confident conviction that God is real and will do what He says. The person who possesses Hebrews 11 faith has already begun enjoying the promises of God as if they have been fulfilled. He or she is convinced to the point of death that God will do and be everything He has ever promised.

The men and women of Hebrews 11 possessed faith in God that was not based on whether He would deliver them from difficulty or death in this life. These men and women were anchored in God's sovereign control. "But as it is, they desire a better country, that is, a heavenly one. Therefore God is not ashamed to be called their God, for he has prepared for them a city" (Hebrews 11:16 ESV).

The type of faith that inducted men and women into the list of Hebrews 11 is not merely belief in God or obedience to Him—though these accomplishments are certainly important. The faith that belonged to the people in Hebrews is characterized by a deep-seeded conviction that God will do everything He has ever promised.

The men and women of Hebrews 11 tasted the great banquet of God long before it was spread out before them.

What should we do with their example?

> *Therefore, since we are surrounded by so great*
> *a cloud of witnesses, let us also lay aside every weight,*
> *and sin which clings so closely, and let us run with*
> *endurance the race that is set before us.*
> HEBREWS 12:1 ESV

God is glorified when our choices in this life are empowered by faith in His promises to us. Perhaps the greatest measure of our faith can be taken by our prayer life. What we do not ask God to do indicates what we do not believe He can accomplish.

We must remember that every impossibility with men is possible with God.

> *For with God nothing shall be impossible.*
> LUKE 1:37 KJV

27.
CRIME 101

"Excellent!" I cried. "Elementary," said he.
THE ADVENTURE OF THE CROOKED MAN

As admiration for Sherlock Holmes has grown through the years, so, too, have the details and myths surrounding the great detective.

Take the deerstalker cap, for instance, seen on every illustration of the great detective. Sherlock Holmes never actually wore the hat in any of Conan Doyle's writing. Also, consider a famous phrase many readers readily associate with Sherlock Holmes:

Elementary, my dear Watson.

These words were never spoken in the canon. "Elementary, my dear Watson" is perhaps the most famous quote associated with the mastermind detective, yet it was never uttered in the pages of Conan Doyle's writing. Holmes does say the words "elementary" and "my dear Watson" often, but never together.

The closest we come to seeing the phrase is an exchange like this one from "The Crooked Man":

"I have the advantage of knowing your habits, my dear Watson," said he. "When your round is a short one you

walk, and when it is a long one you use a hansom. As I
perceive that your boots, although used, are by no means
dirty, I cannot doubt that you are at present busy enough
to justify the hansom."

"Excellent!" I cried.

"Elementary," said he.[1]

Like this signature phrase attributed to the great detective, many of the details and mannerisms employed by actors or artists depicting Sherlock Holmes through the years have actually become absorbed into what we now think of as fact. "Elementary, my dear Watson" is believed to go as far back as a stage play in 1899.

Like so many details surrounding the great detective, discerning readers are left to distinguish fact from myth. So, too, discerning readers of the Bible must distinguish fact from fiction. Some people who genuinely love God get the facts wrong on occasion. Because of this, our knowledge of God and His ways must be biblically informed.

Discernment is an essential component to the Christian life. Discernment is the internal decision-making mechanism that responds to what is seen or heard by carefully applying biblical truth to situations specifically addressed or not addressed in the Bible. Put another way, discernment is the siren that sounds internally when someone says something misleading about God or His Word.

Sometimes people wish to mislead us intentionally:

> *I appeal to you, brothers, to watch out for those*
> *who cause divisions and create obstacles contrary*
> *to the doctrine that you have been taught; avoid them.*
> *For such persons do not serve our Lord Christ,*
> *but their own appetites, and by smooth talk and*
> *flattery they deceive the hearts of the naive.*
> ROMANS 16:17–18 ESV

At other times—and perhaps most often—the misinformation is not intentional. Genuine people can be genuinely wrong.

We must remember that eloquence is never the same thing as accuracy. The scariest, most seductive deceptions are the ones that initially sound good. For instance:

It's okay to be angry with God.

I need to learn to love myself.

God doesn't expect me to live with unfulfilled desires.

No doubt, you can add lies to the list that you have been told when reading religious greeting cards or listening to well-meaning interviewees on Christian radio.

Another prime example: *God wants me to be happy*.

Undiscerning children of God nod in agreement. God loves us, after all, so He certainly wants us to be happy, right? Yet discerning children of God hear the statement and think,

"*Happy* appears fewer than ten times in scripture, and it never speaks in reference to God's desire for my life."

Does God want me to be miserable? Of course not. As my Father, He wants good things for me. But I can rightly assume from looking at the Bible as a whole that God wants certain things for me even more than He wants me to feel optimistic.

God desires my holiness over my happiness.

> *My son, do not lose sight of these—keep sound wisdom and discretion, and they will be life for your soul and adornment for your neck. Then you will walk on your way securely, and your foot will not stumble.*
> PROVERBS 3:21–23 ESV

Being discerning does not mean we should be unkind to people who are incorrect in their application of scripture, nor does it mean we should be inflexible in our dealings with others. As long as we are given breath, we each have growing and learning to do. To that end, every day that I look into the mirror of God's Word and see in it my own need to grow and change, I must be patient with those around me who share the same need.

Discernment means we can't be flexible with people in a way that denies the truths of God. We must listen actively and carefully. Furthermore, we must pray that: "All the words of my mouth are righteous; there is nothing twisted or crooked in them. They are all straight to him who understands, and right to those who find knowledge" (Proverbs 8:8–9 ESV).

We must pray that the work of the Holy Spirit will open the eyes of our understanding.

*Do not be conformed to this world, but be
transformed by the renewal of your mind,
that by testing you may discern what is the will
of God, what is good and acceptable and perfect.*
ROMANS 12:2 ESV

28.

CLASS ACT

"It is my belief, Watson, founded upon my experience,
that the lowest and vilest alleys in London do not
present a more dreadful record of sin than does
the smiling and beautiful countryside."
THE ADVENTURE OF THE COPPER BEECHES

Sherlock Holmes was good at what he did. Once word spread of his masterful skills, his list of clients grew, and so did his need to have eyes and ears all over London.

Holmes was not above using people from all classes of society to help him solve a case. With all the quirks that comprise Holmes' personality—and there are many—his lack of partiality to London's upper or lower class speaks well of him. If there existed any hesitation on the part of the detective to work with anyone, it was members of the upper class who made him think twice, not the lower class.

Though Holmes lived on well-regarded Baker Street, he dealt often and comfortably with those from the worst parts of town.

The *Baker Street Irregulars* were a group of homeless children who appeared in Sherlock Holmes' adventures and were led by an older boy named Wiggins. In Holmes' own words, he hired the Baker Street Irregulars to "go everywhere, see everything, overhear everyone."[1]

Holmes paid the children for their help, plus expenses, to run errands for him. And if they produced information that proved vital to a case, Holmes gave them a bonus.

We first meet the Baker Street Irregulars in *A Study in Scarlet*—the first story that featured the mastermind detective. Because of Conan Doyle's skillful writing, we can easily envision this ragtag team: "He waved his hand, and they scampered away downstairs like so many rats, and we heard their shrill voices next moment in the street."[2]

The Baker Street Irregulars, though a fictional group, represented a difficult reality in Victorian London at the time Conan Doyle was writing. Because of the vast number of homeless families who lived in the streets, many underprivileged children were forced to fend for themselves at a very young age. And because London society paid no attention to these homeless kids, they became virtually invisible, making them perfect miniature detectives who could get whatever information Holmes needed. Holmes made it no secret that he believed one Baker Street Irregular was of more benefit to him than a dozen London police.

Holmes was right when he said that "the lowest and vilest alleys in London do not present a more dreadful record of sin than does the smiling and beautiful countryside."[3]

Biblical truth exists in this secular statement.

For as long as people have walked the earth, self-righteousness has been an epidemic. People have taken pride in where they live or who they know, building their identity around an address, a salary, or a name. Perhaps this vanity compelled John to write, "Everyone who hates his brother is a murderer, and you know that no murderer has eternal life abiding in him" (1 John 3:15 ESV).

John wasn't condoning the larger sin of murder. He was condemning the lesser sin of hatred. He was speaking to the self-righteous who thought highly of themselves for not committing sins like murder while carefully nurturing pet sins like hatred. If murder and hatred are equally egregious, then self-righteousness is a futile enterprise.

In the language of John, there is no such thing as a *larger* or *lesser* sin. Someone who commits murder in the vilest alleys in London is not guiltier of condemnation than someone who hates his brother while living in the smiling and beautiful countryside. Our pride is our own worst enemy because it leads us to believe that who we are is significant in terms of how we should be judged. "Everyone who is arrogant in heart is an abomination to the LORD; be assured, he will not go unpunished" (Proverbs 16:5 ESV).

The point of a statement like the one Holmes made is not to say that no one is sinful. Holmes' job security relied on the sinfulness of people. During the adventures of Sherlock Holmes, he solved cases about blackmail, cheating, fraud, kidnapping, murder, and theft, just to name a few offenses. And still he felt confident saying that sin was not limited to one group or class of people.

In this, he was right. We are all guilty of sinful choices that, when we stand before God, make us equal in our guilt. The holiness of God—as opposed to the comparison of our merits—must be the standard for our conduct. Whether we commit a gross, shocking sin or a socially acceptable misdeed, both are an offense to a holy God. Perhaps this is why God included the sin of pride alongside murder in the list of things He hates. "There are six things that the LORD hates, seven that are an abomination to him: haughty eyes, a lying tongue, and hands that shed innocent blood" (Proverbs 6:16–17 ESV).

It should be noted that consequences may vary and the degrees of punishment may differ, but every sin by every person is always evil.

Thankfully, for each of us there is no sin greater than the forgiveness of God.

For whoever keeps the whole law but fails
in one point has become accountable for all of it.
JAMES 2:10 ESV

29

TRUTH AND CONSEQUENCES

"Any truth is better than indefinite doubt."
THE ADVENTURE OF THE YELLOW FACE

For movie audiences, Sherlock Holmes is as well loved in front of the camera as he is on the printed page. The great detective has been recreated in film so many times that someone studying filmmaking could trace a finger through the history of film production simply by watching the Sherlock Holmes movies in succession.

On May 14, 2012, the Guinness World Records awarded Sherlock Holmes the following honor:

> *Having been depicted on screen 254 times, [Guinness World Records] today announces that Sherlock Holmes, Sir Arthur Conan Doyle's fictional detective, has been awarded a world record for the most portrayed literary human character in film & TV.[1]*

This is yet another impressive honor for the literary hero.

Between the years 1921 and 1923, Stoll Pictures, owned by Sir Oswald Stoll, produced forty-seven films featuring Sherlock Holmes. The films were successful, and Arthur

Conan Doyle gave them his stamp of approval, saying, "My only criticism of the films is that they introduce telephones, motorcars and other luxuries of which the Victorian Holmes never dreamed."[2]

Despite this critique, the films are a valuable piece of Sherlockian history. The events of Sherlock Holmes, as written by Conan Doyle, supposedly take place over the years 1880 to 1914. The Stoll Pictures films were made between the years 1921 to 1923 in the London streets where Sherlock Holmes lived and worked.

So the early twentieth-century backdrop in the Stoll films is the real deal. Watching these films, a viewer could see Sherlock Holmes in the years he was theoretically alive and working. No twenty-first-century movie studio could recreate the movies to be any more realistic. Watching the films, then, despite the seven-year gap between the end of Holmes' adventures and the start of the films, allows the viewer to feel as if he is observing Sherlock Holmes in his natural habitat.

Holmes loved facts more than anything else. To his mind, separating facts and feelings was one of the greatest rules of basic investigation. For instance, in "The Adventure of the Yellow Face," Holmes and Dr. Watson return to 221B Baker Street after taking a walk, only to discover that someone has come and gone, leaving a pipe behind. Holmes picks it up, taps it, and says:

"Pipes are occasionally of extraordinary interest. Nothing has more individuality, save perhaps watches and bootlaces. The indications here, however, are neither very marked nor very important. The owner is obviously a muscular man, left-handed, with an excellent set of teeth, careless in his habits, and with no need to practise economy."[3]

As usual, Holmes was spot-on in his deductions.

Holmes was able to approach a piece of evidence, separate facts from feelings, and arrive at truth. He was quoted in "The Adventure of the Yellow Face" as saying, "Any truth is better than infinite doubt."[4]

No truer words were ever spoken.

As Christians, we must be driven by our desire to know the truth about God. John 18 bears witness to one of the most intense moments in the life of Christ. Jesus is brought before Pilate and questioned about his identity, and the following conversation ensues:

Then Pilate said to him, "So you are a king?" Jesus answered, "You say that I am a king. For this purpose I was born and for this purpose I have come into the world— to bear witness to the truth. Everyone who is of the truth listens to my voice." Pilate said to him, "What is truth?"
JOHN 18:37–38 ESV

What is truth?

Believers and nonbelievers alike have been asking this question for centuries. Dinner tables and debate teams have erupted over the truth of God. College professors and political parties have clashed over the truth of the Gospel. People groups and sovereign states have divided over the truth of Jesus Christ.

"Jesus said to him, 'I am the way, and the truth, and the life. No one comes to the Father except through me'" (John 14:6 ESV). If God had only given us John 14:6, we would have enough to trust Him with our lives. In His kindness, He has given us the entire Word of God, full of the truth that sets us free. Still, the question exists:

Why does truth matter so much?

The short answer: those who do not know and love the truth will spend an eternity separated from God.

And then the lawless one will be revealed, whom the Lord Jesus will kill with the breath of his mouth and bring to nothing by the appearance of his coming. The coming of the lawless one is by the activity of Satan with all power and false signs and wonders, and with all wicked deception for those who are perishing, because they refused to love the truth and so be saved. Therefore God sends them a strong delusion, so that they may believe what is false, in order that all may

be condemned who did not believe the truth
but had pleasure in unrighteousness.
2 THESSALONIANS 2:8–12 ESV

God's goal for man from the beginning of time is that man would know the truth. Christ came into the world to bear witness to the truth of God. Creation itself, according to Romans 1, was created to bear witness to the truth of God so that we are without excuse.

We must be relentless in pursuing the truth. This means we must study God's Word in search of truth. We must challenge everything we hear and everything we think we know by looking into God's Word for the answers. We must then speak this truth to ourselves and others.

Finally, we should "proclaim Him, admonishing every man and teaching every man with all wisdom, so that we may present every man complete in Christ" (Colossians 1:28 NASB).

Nothing matters more in this life than the truth of God.

"And you will know the truth,
and the truth will set you free."
JOHN 8:32 NLT

30.

THE MORIARTY EFFECT

*"I may tell you that Moriarty rules with a rod
of iron over his people. There is only one
punishment in his code. It is death."*
THE VALLEY OF FEAR

Sherlock Holmes met his match in Professor James Moriarty. What Holmes was to justice, Moriarty was to crime. They were two sides of the same coin—the classic hero and villain. According to Holmes:

> *"[Moriarty] is the organizer of half that is evil and of nearly all that is undetected in this great city. He is a genius, a philosopher, an abstract thinker. He has a brain of the first order. He sits motionless, like a spider in the center of its web, but that web has a thousand radiations, and he knows well every quiver of each of them."[1]*

Even though Moriarty was the brains of his organization, he used a well-organized band of yes-men to carry out his plans.

> *"He does little himself. He only plans. But his agents are numerous and splendidly organized. If there is a crime to*

be done, a paper to be abstracted, we will say, a house to
be rifled, a man to be removed—the word is passed to
the Professor, the matter is organized and carried out."²

Even the careful organization of his crime ring showcased Moriarty's superior intelligence. In using agents to do his bidding, he would never be caught, if he were even suspected of any wrongdoing.

Holmes always suspected Moriarty of wrongdoing.

Moriarty was behind some of the most baffling crimes confronting Holmes. For as often as Moriarty was mentioned, he was rarely seen in the canon—showing up in only two stories: "The Final Problem" and *The Valley of Fear.* The professor was mentioned, though not seen, in only five other stories. And yet, despite his rare appearance on the page, he maintained a consistent presence in the canon, so that readers were always looking for his fingerprints in every crime.

Moriarty worked behind the scenes as silently and effectively as the great detective—leading some readers to believe they knew what Holmes would look like if he fought for evil instead of justice.

Of all the villains in the canon—and there were many—none were as feared as Moriarty. The evil professor was capable of keeping the great detective on his toes in a way that no one else could. Holmes devoted the better part of his energy to destroying Moriarty. At times, he was obsessed with this mission, willing to destroy himself if it meant taking Moriarty down with him.

So it is for Christians. We each have our own Moriarty.

And you were dead in the trespasses and sins in which you once walked, following the course of this world, following the prince of the power of the air, the spirit that is now at work in the sons of disobedience—among whom we all once lived in the passions of our flesh, carrying out the desires of the body and the mind, and were by nature children of wrath, like the rest of mankind.
EPHESIANS 2:1–3 ESV

Just as Holmes remained suspicious of Moriarty, so, too, we should be vigilant to guard ourselves from the world, the flesh, and the devil. As a means to this end, we must be certain never to think we can handle any sin on our own.

The quickest way to view sin the way that we should is to fear God the way that we should.

Each of us knows where our private pitfalls and personal limitations exist. For some it might be lust; for others it may be complaining. Regardless of where our strongest temptations lie, we must battle temptation at all cost. Mindlessly flipping channels on the television or speaking without thinking when among friends, for instance, will not aid in the struggle against lust or complaint.

A character like Professor Moriarty lends itself easily to an object lesson about the devil. Moriarty does sound a lot like the evil one, no doubt about it. But it is possible that we can become so vigilant to protect ourselves from whom we perceive Satan to be that we miss the threat of our own sinful flesh. The truth is, *we* are capable of doing terrible things if left to our own devices. "Whoever makes a practice of sinning is of the devil, for the devil has been sinning from the beginning. The reason the Son of God appeared was to destroy the works of the devil" (1 John 3:8 ESV).

Just as Holmes constantly looked over his shoulder for any sign of Moriarty's shadow, so, too, we should watch for sin's snares, understanding that the origin of temptation is the lust of our own hearts.

Note to self: between every temptation and the decision to sin is a choice. Being tempted, then, is not the same as doing wrong. We must pray for God to help us stand firm in the face of our weakness.

Thankfully, the Gospel exists for our failures.

The thief comes only to steal and kill and destroy.
I came that they may have life and have it abundantly.
JOHN 10:10 ESV

31.

THE MASTER PLAN

"What is the meaning of it, Watson? What object is
served by this circle of misery and violence and fear?
It must tend to some end, or else our universe is
ruled by chance, which is unthinkable."
THE ADVENTURE OF THE CARDBOARD BOX

Whether or not Sherlock Holmes believed in God is an issue that has long been a matter of debate. Because he is a fictional character, the answer technically has no consequence. Fictional characters were not created by God and will not live forever with Him. Even still, some readers wish to understand if it was Arthur Conan Doyle's desire for Sherlock Holmes to believe in God. The canon is not silent on the issue of religion.

In "The Boscombe Valley Mystery," Holmes is hired, for the first time, to investigate a crime that happened outside of London. A landowner has been killed, and it is now up to Holmes to wade through secrets and corruption to determine the culprit. The final scene in the story is a powerful one in which the guilty man confesses to the great detective. At the end of the story, Holmes arrives at a passionate conclusion:

"God help us!" said Holmes after a long silence. "Why
does fate play such tricks with poor, helpless worms? I

never hear of such a case as this that I do not think of
Baxter's words, and say, 'There, but for the grace of God,
goes Sherlock Holmes.' "[1]

This paragraph and others like it spark debates as to the mastermind's belief in the Master. These words are also reminiscent of Paul's words in the New Testament:

But by the grace of God I am what I am, and his
grace toward me was not in vain. On the contrary,
I worked harder than any of them, though it was
not I, but the grace of God that is with me.
1 Corinthians 15:10 esv

We do not have sufficient evidence to know what Sherlock Holmes believed about God, but it doesn't really matter. Whether Holmes' creator, Arthur Conan Doyle, trusted Christ for salvation is an entirely different and altogether more important issue.

According to researchers, Conan Doyle was born into a Catholic family and went to school with the Jesuits. By the time he enrolled in medical school, by his own admission he had rejected the concept of God. This is tragic news for the soul of Conan Doyle, proving talent and intelligence alone do not merit salvation.

It takes more than a passive interest in God to receive salvation from Him.

At the time Conan Doyle was writing about his famous detective, a man named Charles Darwin was alive and well, becoming influential in Victorian scientific study. No doubt Conan Doyle was familiar with Darwin—and vice versa— even as Conan Doyle wrote the canon. Darwin, like Doyle, grew up in a religious family where he went to church every week and attended a religious school. Before investing his life in the subjects he would best be remembered for—among them, evolution and atheism—he intended to become a clergyman.

Darwin, writing about his disbelief in God, said:

Thus disbelief crept over me at a very slow rate, but was at last complete. The rate was so slow that I felt no distress, and have never since doubted even for a single second that my conclusion was correct.[2]

If history bears an accurate record, Conan Doyle and Charles Darwin did not believe the Gospel. What is the Gospel? The good news that Jesus Christ paid the price of sin and suffering so that we could enjoy fellowship with God for eternity. "For God has not destined us for wrath, but to obtain salvation through our Lord Jesus Christ, who died for us so that whether we are awake or asleep we might live with him" (1 Thessalonians 5:9–10 ESV).

We live in an age where we are taught that God, like a

benevolent grandfather, will be pleased to accept whatever we have to offer Him. No longer is it politically correct to say that Jesus Christ is the only way to God. Words like *intolerant* and *narrow-minded* exist for those who believe that Jesus is the only way. We are a society that avoids commitment in all areas, including faith.

The truth is, God is intolerant of sin and He is narrow-minded as it pertains to life eternal:

> *"Enter by the narrow gate. For the gate is wide and the way is easy that leads to destruction, and those who enter by it are many. For the gate is narrow and the way is hard that leads to life, and those who find it are few."*
> MATTHEW 7:13–14 ESV

As children of God, we are never called to be unkind to nonbelievers, nor are we expected to singlehandedly change the hearts and minds of those who can only be changed by Him. Yet we must understand that a person's passing interest in religious matters is not the equivalent of a right relationship with God.

We must humbly and diligently share the truth that Jesus alone is the way to God.

Jesus answered, "I am the way and the truth and the life.
No one comes to the Father except through me."
JOHN 14:6 NIV

32.

THE MIND'S EYE

*"Let us walk in these beautiful woods
and give a few hours to the birds and flowers."*
THE ADVENTURE OF BLACK PETER

Something strange happened in "The Adventure of the Naval Treaty."

Holmes, the least sentimental detective on the planet, interrupts his investigation of a case to discuss a moss rose. And in one of the most beautiful monologues in the canon, Holmes demonstrates his incredible skills of deductive reasoning—or reasoning that moves from observation to hypothesis—when he says:

> *"What a lovely thing a rose is!"*
>
> *He walked past the couch to the open window and held up the drooping stalk of a moss-rose, looking down at the dainty blend of crimson and green. It was a new phase of his character to me, for I had never before seen him show any keen interest in natural objects.[1]*

And then Holmes says:

*"There is nothing in which deduction is so necessary
as in religion," said he, leaning with his back against
the shutters. "It can be built up as an exact science by
the reasoner. Our highest assurance of the goodness
of Providence seems to me to rest in the flowers. All
other things, our powers, our desires, our food, are all
really necessary for our existence in the first instance.
But this rose is extra. Its smell and its colour are an
embellishment of life, not a condition of it. It is only
goodness which gives extras, and so I say again that we
have much to hope from the flowers."[2]*

Holmes, or perhaps more specifically Conan Doyle, inadvertently delivered a peculiar lecture on the existence of God. Whether or not Doyle was acquainted with Romans 1 as he wrote "The Naval Treaty," he offered a subtle nod to the following words of scripture:

*For what can be known about God is plain to them,
because God has shown it to them. For his invisible
attributes, namely, his eternal power and divine
nature, have been clearly perceived, ever since the
creation of the world, in the things that have
been made. So they are without excuse.*
ROMANS 1:19–20 ESV

In his first novel, *A Study in Scarlet*, Holmes explained:

> *"From a drop of water a logician could infer the possibility of an Atlantic or a Niagara without having seen or heard of one or the other. So all life is a great chain, the nature of which is known whenever we are shown a single link of it."*[3]

Many of us who have tasted salvation for a stretch of years have inevitably wrestled with the questions, *But what about the people who are never told about God? How can they possibly be held accountable to Him?* In asking these questions, we may envision tiny people groups living in the jungles or untouched valleys of the world. Our minds may travel to the people who lived in the Amazonian region of Ecuador—the group for whom Jim Elliot and his four companions gave their lives.

What about them? Without a copy of the scriptures, what will they ever learn about God?

According to Romans 1, we can be certain God designed us to know He exists. In every person's heart, he or she knows we are accountable to someone. This passage teaches us that God created the universe in such a way to make it clear to us who He is and whom we should worship as a result. God is so confident that His creation accomplishes this purpose that He holds us responsible if we fail to put faith in Him.

His confidence should warrant ours. His goodness should motivate us to share the good news of the Gospel: We have all sinned. The consequence of our sin is death. Christ died for our sin—providing the only release from its eternal bondage. We can be saved from eternal death by placing our faith in Jesus Christ.

One of the kindest things God does for His creation is allow us to look at a rose or a drop of water and know instinctively that Someone made those things, *that Somebody made us*. God was not obligated to create the world in such a way that we would know He exists. Yet He did.

> *The heavens declare the glory of God, and the sky above proclaims his handiwork. Day to day pours out speech, and night to night reveals knowledge. There is no speech, nor are there words, whose voice is not heard.*
> PSALM 19:1–3 ESV

What amazing grace!

Romans 1 reveals three truths to which each of us will stand accountable. First, God made us. Second, we are sinners. Third, we will answer to our Creator.

Let's be prepared. And to the extent that we are able, let's help others prepare to meet God.

> *For since the creation of the world God's invisible qualities—his eternal power and divine nature—have been clearly seen, being understood from what has been made, so that people are without excuse.*
> ROMANS 1:20 NIV

33.

THE GRAND FINALE

*"I assure you, my good Lastrade, that I have
an excellent reason for everything that I do."*
THE ADVENTURE OF THE NORWOOD BUILDER

Arthur Conan Doyle had no intention of publishing his detective stories in *Beeton's Christmas Annual*—a brightly covered paperback magazine filled with advertisements and stories. It sold for a shilling—the equivalent of a few pennies—and always sold out before Christmas.

When Doyle couldn't convince any other publishers to buy *A Study in Scarlet* from him, he settled on *Beeton's Christmas Annual*, in its twenty-eighth season, and later said of the decision: "When my little Holmes book began also to do the circular tour I was hurt, for I knew that it deserved a better fate."[1]

It was in the pages of the little Christmas paperback annual that fans of the great detective were first introduced to Sherlock Holmes and his friend, Dr. Watson—the two of whom would take the criminal world by storm. Soon enough, though, Conan Doyle's stories would be serialized in *The Strand Magazine*, a monthly magazine filled with short fiction and general interest pieces.

It was for *The Strand Magazine* that Sidney Paget provided the illustrations of Sherlock Holmes that would finally give readers a glimpse of the mastermind detective and his colorful cast of characters. Paget based his illustrations of the great detective on his brother, Walter, so closely that pictures of Walter Paget are essentially photos of Sherlock Holmes.

By the time Doyle published *The Hound of the Baskervilles*, readers were lined up outside *The Strand Magazine*'s office eagerly waiting to receive their copy of the installment. *A Study in Scarlet* would eventually receive the better fate of which Conan Doyle originally dreamed.

Interesting to note, the original November 1887 copy of *Beeton's Christmas Annual* which contains *A Study in Scarlet* is now considered to be the most expensive magazine in the world. In 2007, a copy auctioned for $156,000. Had faithful *Beeton's Christmas Annual* readers understood its destiny in 1887, perhaps they would have spent a couple extra shillings and put a few mint condition copies away for future generations. And maybe Conan Doyle wouldn't have felt so betrayed by its original publication.

Sherlock Holmes would go on to demonstrate many interesting habits throughout the canon—some good and some bad—one of them involving the way he liked to conclude a case. He loved to withhold a critical fact that would change everything about the investigation. He would cling to this hidden bit of information the way a child might grasp a toy behind his back, waiting for the right chance to showcase the knowledge—and in Holmes' case—the resolution to the entire investigation.

In "The Adventure of the Naval Treaty" Holmes admits, "Watson here will tell you that I never can resist a touch of the dramatic."[2] This may be one of the greatest understatements in the adventures of Sherlock Holmes. The great detective appreciated a good finale.

So, too, as Christians, we understand the promise of a fantastic conclusion.

No matter how twisted a situation gets or how bad a complication appears to be, we know we have a God in heaven who is carefully working the details together for our good and His glory. No job loss, broken relationship, or cancer diagnosis has ever had the last word for a child of God. This world is not the last chapter for those who know Him.

For my thoughts are not your thoughts, neither are your ways my ways, declares the LORD. For as the heavens are higher than the earth, so are my ways higher than your ways and my thoughts than your thoughts.
ISAIAH 55:8–9 ESV

With a perfect love for His children, our heavenly Father loves to orchestrate the circumstances in our life such that the resolution to our story is more splendid than anything we could possibly imagine. Unlike the fictional detective, however, God doesn't withhold the resolution for dramatic purposes. In fact, He tells us to rest assured that He will resolve everything in the end. "And we know that for those who love God all things work together for good, for those who are called according to his purpose" (Romans 8:28 ESV).

The fact that God will accomplish His will in our lives is as certain as our salvation. Though it is important to notice it says "we know" and not "we understand." God never promises we will make sense of the winding path that leads to life eternal. But He promises that when it all works out in the end, we will marvel again at the goodness of God in our lives. We can be confident that God always has our best interests in mind.

If you are a child of God, all of His plans for you are only and always good.

In him we have obtained an inheritance, having been predestined according to the purpose of him who works all things according to the counsel of his will.
EPHESIANS 1:11 ESV

34.

SURVIVAL GUIDE

There is nothing more stimulating than a
case where everything goes against you.
THE HOUND OF THE BASKERVILLES

Conan Doyle's first story, *A Study in Scarlet*, was initially a failure. In hindsight, writing the adventures of Sherlock Holmes was an incredibly successful endeavor for Doyle. His popularity spans three centuries and is still going strong. But it doesn't change the fact:

Sherlock Holmes almost flopped.

As has been the case for many successful authors throughout literary history, Conan Doyle's *A Study in Scarlet* was rejected by several publishers before, in desperation, he finally sold the rights for pocket change. He took up writing in the first place because he needed help to make ends meet.

Though *A Study in Scarlet* has achieved enormous success since its publication, it is arguably one of Conan Doyle's weakest stories about the great detective. Among the list of complaints, Conan Doyle committed the cardinal sin of withholding from the reader vital information necessary to solve the mystery.

Conan Doyle's second novel, *The Sign of Four*, struggled

as well, and Doyle became discouraged. Thinking Sherlock Holmes was doomed to failure, the author turned his attention to another project—writing a play called *Angels of Darkness*—that wouldn't be published until 2001, almost seventy years after his death.

Had Conan Doyle's biography been written after his second novel, *The Sign of Four*, Sherlock Holmes would tell a different tale. We likely would not know the name Arthur Conan Doyle. He would have joined the ranks of those who stopped trying too soon.

It must have been from a bit of personal experience, then, that Doyle wrote the following line in *The Hound of Baskervilles*: "There is nothing more stimulating than a case where everything goes against you."[1] When the odds are stacked against us, we have nothing to lose and everything to gain.

The Hound of the Baskervilles is the third novel written by Doyle and is listed as the top Conan Doyle novel—receiving a rare, perfect 100 from Sherlockian scholars. The BBC includes it on the UK list of 200 best-loved novels.[2] Had Doyle given up after writing *A Study in Scarlet* or *The Sign of Four*, there would be no third novel.

Conan Doyle knew what it was like to pound the pavement and come up lacking. He also knew what it was like to persevere until a difficult, personal goal was accomplished. His writing is now translated into more than eighty languages, including Czech, Egyptian, Greek, and Urdu.

As Christians, we could learn a thing or two about perseverance from Conan Doyle. As believers, we should strive to give personal testimony to persevering with the grace of God in every goal that is good and Christ honoring. This isn't to say that our lives will be easy or happy all the time or that we won't consider giving up on a regular basis.

Scripturally speaking, if the Christian life is not hard, we are doing something wrong. The Bible speaks often about overcoming difficulty in the battle for perseverance:

Be joyful in hope, patient in affliction, faithful in prayer.
Romans 12:12 niv

Let us not become weary in doing good, for at the proper time we will reap a harvest if we do not give up.
Galatians 6:9 niv

Blessed is the one who perseveres under trial because, having stood the test, that person will receive the crown of life that the Lord has promised to those who love him.
James 1:12 niv

If the Christian life were meant to be effortless, the Bible would encourage us to relax as opposed to endure. It would tell us to sleep instead of fight. The very language of the scriptures indicates that the Christian life will be challenging. But it will be worth it.

Important to understand: persevering in the Christian life does not mean living flawlessly; it means fighting hard. *Fighting what?* Sin, temptation, the devil, and our flesh. "Dear friends, I urge you, as foreigners and exiles, to abstain from sinful desires, which wage war against your soul" (1 Peter 2:11 NIV).

Thankfully, we do not need to persevere alone. Charles Spurgeon, in a sermon entitled "Justification by Grace," said, "If He gives you the grace to make you believe, He will give you the grace to live a holy life afterwards."[3]

God will empower us to persevere. This is great assurance. The significance of depending on God and not self for perseverance is that He is responsible to provide everything we need to live holy, godly lives in this world.

Don't give up on the goals God has impressed on you to accomplish. Don't join the ranks of those who stopped trying too soon. God gave His Son for us. We can therefore be confident that He will give us anything else we need to live for Him.

> *What, then, shall we say in response to these things?*
> *If God is for us, who can be against us?*
> ROMANS 8:31 NIV

35.

BALANCING ACT

"Weakness in one limb is often compensated
for by exceptional strength in the others."
THE ADVENTURES OF SHERLOCK HOLMES

A strange thing happened after Dr. Watson became room-mates with Sherlock Holmes. They began to work well to-gether and even enjoy each other's company. Ordinarily this might not be noteworthy, except the brilliant detective had the social skills of a hermit crab.

In the second chapter of Conan Doyle's first novel, *A Study in Scarlet*, Watson says, "As the weeks went by, my interest in him and my curiosity as to his aims in life grad-ually deepened and increased."[1] Where most of us would have spent a week living with the great detective and gone running for the hills, Dr. Watson merely became more interested in the detective's strange ways.

By the second chapter of Doyle's first novel about the pair, Watson and Holmes were picking up each other's slack and completing each other's sentences. Throughout the canon, the two advocated each other's strengths and balanced each other's weaknesses. They demonstrated what it is like to be two people of one mind, even though the two men were as different as night and day. Holmes and Watson had things to teach each other and offer each other.

Had the fictional pair been alike instead of different, the crime-solving team would have failed. Each had something valuable to offer the other.

We should pursue this type of no-holds-barred unity with our brothers and sisters in the church. Each of us, if we know Christ as our Savior, belongs to the body of Christ. As such, our membership to our local, Bible-believing church is one of the most important aspects of our lives. Too often the church is viewed simply as a social club or a place to fellowship with friends on the weekend. As such, we can take it or leave it, depending on how we feel at the time or what other obligations might be more pressing.

This is not God's plan. The church is much more important than any social engagement.

We have a role to fill in the church that is as unique as we are. At the same time, we have an opportunity to lay aside our personal initiatives and idiosyncrasies in favor of worshipping God with the people of God. On earth, we have no greater privilege.

Therefore God has highly exalted him and bestowed on him the name that is above every name, so that at the name of Jesus every knee should bow, in heaven and on earth and under the earth, and every tongue confess that

Jesus Christ is Lord, to the glory of God the Father.
PHILIPPIANS 2:9–11 ESV

In no other institution are we accepted purely because of what we believe and whom we worship. The body of Christ, biblically speaking, cannot discriminate on the basis of age, class, race, language, ability, gender, or intelligence. It cannot discriminate on the basis of these characteristics because God does not discriminate on the basis of these characteristics. "For God so loved the world, that he gave his only Son, that whoever believes in him should not perish but have eternal life" (John 3:16 ESV).

The church matters infinitely more than our personal agendas. The church is not a *what*, but a *who*. The church is the collective, chosen children of God.

But you are a chosen race, a royal priesthood,
a holy nation, a people for his own possession,
that you may proclaim the excellencies of him who
called you out of darkness into his marvelous light.
1 PETER 2:9 ESV

To this end, we each matter as parts of the whole. We should advocate each other's strengths and balance each other's weaknesses. We should demonstrate to a watching world what it is like to be multiple people of one mind, even though we are as different as is humanly possible. We have things to teach each other and offer one another as one cohesive witness in the world.

Think of the most difficult members in your church. They aren't the enemy. They are your ministry. If they know Christ, they are your brothers and sisters. Advocate for them. Balance them. Aim to love them in the Lord.

We each have a place in the body of Christ. We cannot be false judges of God's standard—that is, we should not try to decide who is worthy of our time or care in the body of Christ. In the words of the New Testament, we should seek to encourage one another and build each other up (see 1 Thessalonians 5:11).

The Gospel requires that we love each other in the body of Christ, working together to accomplish good for God's glory.

> *We are many parts of one body,*
> *and we all belong to each other.*
> ROMANS 12:5 NLT

FOR THE LOVE

"We can't command our love,
but we can our actions."
THE ADVENTURES OF SHERLOCK HOLMES

Sherlock Holmes called Irene Adler *the woman*.[1]

Adler, who, according to Holmes, is "the daintiest thing under a bonnet on the planet,"[2] is an American opera singer who was embroiled in a scandal with the King of Bohemia. Also according to Holmes, Adler was the only woman who ever outsmarted him.

Holmes' simple nickname for Adler sets readers' imaginations ablaze, causing students and fans of the detective to wonder for over a century if Holmes was in love with *the woman*. Romantics have often tried to link Adler and Holmes, presenting Adler as *the woman who got away*. Others maintain Adler was *the woman who stole the detective's heart*.

So much goes unsaid about *the woman*.

Holmes encounters Adler in "A Scandal in Bohemia" when he works to thwart a public scandal involving the king. Holmes describes Adler as "a lovely woman, with a face that a man might die for," and that sentiment is all any literary dreamer needs to make more of the relationship between the two than actually exists on the page.

Despite only appearing in one short story, Adler is the second most notable female character in the stories of Sherlock Holmes, the first being Mrs. Hudson.

Nothing else in Conan Doyle's writing implies that Holmes maintained anything for Adler beyond a deep appreciation for her rich intelligence. It would appear Holmes referred to her as *the woman* because she was the only woman ever to have beaten him in a pursuit. And since Holmes did not generally respect the intellect of women, Adler's accomplishment must have impressed him.

Ask casual readers for the name of Holmes' love interest, however, and wait for the response: *Irene Adler*.

Some readers refuse to believe anything else. Still others can't appreciate a good storyline without a love interest. Whatever the case, the outcome does not change the fact that Holmes and Adler never met again in the pages of the canon.

Love is a funny thing. Some can't live with it, and others can't live without it. Where Christian love is concerned, the choice is not ours to make.

Children of God have the obligation to love one another as Christ loves us. In fact, according to Romans 13, loving our neighbor fulfills the requirements of God's law.

Owe no one anything, except to love each other,
for the one who loves another has fulfilled the law.

For the commandments, "You shall not commit adultery,
You shall not murder, You shall not steal, You shall not
covet," and any other commandment, are summed
up in this word: "You shall love your neighbor as
yourself." Love does no wrong to a neighbor;
therefore love is the fulfilling of the law.
ROMANS 13:8–10 ESV

Interesting, isn't it, that we often try to make fulfilling God's law about so many other things when it is as simple as loving someone. If we love someone, we won't sin against *Him.*

Put on then, as God's chosen ones, holy and beloved,
compassionate hearts, kindness, humility, meekness,
and patience, bearing with one another and, if one has
a complaint against another, forgiving each other;
as the Lord has forgiven you, so you also must forgive.
And above all these put on love, which binds
everything together in perfect harmony.
COLOSSIANS 3:12–14 ESV

Anyone who has been a Christian for a while knows the obligation: love the Lord your God with all your heart, soul, and mind; and love your neighbor as yourself (Luke 10:27). But the road map to accomplishing the goal is not so clear. *What is this type of love? What is my obligation? Who is my neighbor?*

The questions are not unique to our generation.

In Luke 10, a sincere, zealous lawyer asks Jesus the question, "Who is my neighbor?" He may have been expecting Jesus to offer a simple definition or provide a specific list. Instead, what the lawyer receives is a story—Jesus shares the parable of the Good Samaritan.

The story of the Good Samaritan teaches us, among other truths, that we don't need to look for people to love. Real people with real stories who need the real love of Jesus cross our path every day. And when we encounter these individuals—whether the person is a member of the religious elite or whether he has been beaten and left for dead at the side of the road—we are invited, even sovereignly ordered— to demonstrate the love of God. "Therefore be imitators of God, as beloved children. And walk in love, as Christ loved us and gave himself up for us, a fragrant offering and sacrifice to God" (Ephesians 5:1–2 ESV).

The love of God flows most naturally through a network of existing relationships. This type of love isn't always easy. Sometimes showing love means being compassionate in the face of obnoxious prejudice or deliberate unkindness. Sometimes showing love comes at great cost or with excessive discomfort. What motivates us to love in these moments of frustration and hurt? *God's love.* We who have been forgiven much are equipped to love much.

Passion is not a dominant ingredient in the stories of

Sherlock Holmes, and neither is it in biblical love. Though God loves His children zealously—no question about it—passion as a strong emotion or feeling is not the driving force behind His actions. He is not motivated by feelings the way we often are. He does not love me because I am loveable. He loves me because He is the God of love.

This is good news. This means nothing I do will make Him love me any more or any less.

One thing is certain for the child of God: Love is not optional.

> *Owe nothing to anyone—except for your obligation*
> *to love one another. If you love your neighbor,*
> *you will fulfill the requirements of God's law.*
> ROMANS 13:8 NLT

37.

DEATH GRIP

*"Problems may be solved in the study which
have baffled all those who have sought a
solution by the aid of their senses."*
THE FIVE ORANGE PIPS

One characteristic of Sherlock Holmes that often goes un-mentioned is his impressive strength. No doubt, with all of his other extraordinary traits and talents, the detective's physical strength isn't particularly noteworthy. Nevertheless, Dr. Watson takes note of it in the canon.

In "The Adventure of the Speckled Band," we observe a man named Dr. Grimesby Roylott confronting the great detective who is investigating the mysterious death of Roylott's stepdaughter. He pays the detective an unpleasant visit:

"I will go when I have said my say. Don't you dare to meddle with my affairs. I know that Miss Stoner has been here. I traced her! I am a dangerous man to fall foul of! See here."

He stepped swiftly forward, seized the poker, and bent it into a curve with his huge brown hands. "See that you keep yourself out of my grip," he snarled, and hurling the twisted poker into the fireplace he strode out of the room.[1]

Roylott is described as "a huge man that framed the doorway. So tall was he that his hat actually brushed the cross bar of the doorway, and his breadth seemed to span it across from side to side." So what we know of Roylott is nearly the opposite of what we know about Holmes from a previous description in *A Study in Scarlet*: "In height he was rather over six feet, and so excessively lean that he seemed to be considerably taller."[2] In an effort to scare Holmes off from investigating the case further, Roylott picks up a fire poker and bends it in half before marching out the door. And what was Sherlock Holmes' reaction to this intimidation? Did he quake in fear or tremble in the shadows of 221B Baker Street? Hardly. According to Watson:

> *"He seems a very amiable person," said Holmes, laughing. "I am not quite so bulky, but if he had remained I might have shown him that my grip was not much more feeble than his own." As he spoke he picked up the steel poker and, with a sudden effort, straightened it out again.[3]*

The lean detective proved a match for Hercules.

This demonstration of strength by Sherlock Holmes was not an isolated event. In another story, "The Yellow Face," Dr.

Watson describes Holmes, saying, "Few men were capable of greater muscular effort."[4]

It would seem—in the face of his other impressive abilities—Holmes' strength is often and easily overlooked, but it is there nonetheless. So it is for those of us who know and love God's Word.

As children in Sunday school, many of us learned the song "Jesus Loves Me." No doubt entire years of our toddlerhood were spent rehearsing the line, "We are weak, but He is strong." And yet, even after years of singing the truth, we struggle to let its implications take root in our hearts.

God's strength, to us, can be often and easily overlooked. We talk about many of God's other attributes freely—His love, His mercy, His grace—but we stumble over the aspect of His strength. Perhaps we cannot truly comprehend it. Even the greatest imaginations certainly come up short when compared to reality.

Who has measured the waters in the hollow of his
hand and marked off the heavens with a span, enclosed
the dust of the earth in a measure and weighed the
mountains in scales and the hills in a balance?
ISAIAH 40:12 ESV

The strongest man is no match for the might of God. And this God who laid the foundations of the earth is interested in the details of our lives.

We don't believe it. Not really. Otherwise we wouldn't act like God is weak and we are strong. If we really believed in the limitless strength of God, we would go to Him first in prayer instead of as a last resort. We would ask Him for everything we need instead of trying to get it ourselves. We wouldn't shudder in fear over the threats of men or wonder in vain how our needs would be met.

If we truly believed in the power of God, we would embrace our own weakness. Consider these words from Paul:

> *Three times I pleaded with the Lord about this, that it should leave me. But he said to me, "My grace is sufficient for you, for my power is made perfect in weakness." Therefore I will boast all the more gladly of my weaknesses, so that the power of Christ may rest upon me. For the sake of Christ, then, I am content with weaknesses, insults, hardships, persecutions, and calamities. For when I am weak, then I am strong.*
> 2 Corinthians 12:8–10 esv

More than our weaknesses, our delusions of strength get in the way of true success. When we catch a glimpse of how weak we actually are, we go to God and ask for help. We say with the psalmist: "My flesh and my heart may fail, but God is the strength of my heart and my portion forever" (Psalm 73:26 esv).

When we believe we are strong, we don't go to God in prayer. We don't cling to the precious promises in His Word. We don't comfort ourselves with the songs that communicate the truths of His character.

In short, when we believe we are strong, we don't avail ourselves of His strength. When we understand we are weak, His power is made perfect in us.

> *"No eye has seen, no ear has heard,*
> *and no mind has imagined what God*
> *has prepared for those who love him."*
> 1 CORINTHIANS 2:9 NLT

38.

NEXT TO GODLINESS

"We can but try."
THE ADVENTURE OF THE CREEPING MAN

Sherlock Holmes was a slob. Or was he?

According to Dr. Watson, Sherlock Holmes "is an eccentric, with no regard for contemporary standards of tidiness or good order."[1] However, Watson later describes the great detective as "having a cat-like love of personal cleanliness."[2]

In "The Adventure of the Musgrave Ritual," Watson again alludes to Holmes' messy habits, saying:

> *Although in his methods of thought he was the neatest and most methodical of mankind. . .[he] keeps his cigars in the coal-scuttle, his tobacco in the toe end of a Persian slipper, and his unanswered correspondence transfixed by a jack-knife into the very centre of his wooden mantelpiece. . . He had a horror of destroying documents . . . . Thus month after month his papers accumulated, until every corner of the room was stacked with bundles of manuscript which were on no account to be burned, and which could not be put away save by their owner.[3]*

So which is it? Is Holmes a slob or isn't he?

Yes. And no.

This may be yet another example of Conan Doyle failing to fact-check and jumbling the details of his literary world. Or, perhaps more realistically, this could be an example of how things work in real life.

Do you ever feel this way? That perhaps one day you have mastered something and the next you are starting from square one?—that the things which comprise your greatest strengths are also, at times, your worst struggles?

Consider the following questions:

Are you a vibrant, growing Christian? *Yes. And no.*

Do you maintain healthy Bible reading and prayer habits? *Yes. And no.*

Do you abstain from sin? *Yes. And no.*

Depending on the season of life and even, sometimes, depending on the day, the answers can become complicated. A brief snapshot of our life at different times could reveal what appear to be entirely different people.

The unfortunate truth is that there is no quick path to growth. Growth in Christ is a messy endeavor. We'd like to believe we pray a saving prayer and achieve sanctification before saying *amen.* Unfortunately, Christian maturity doesn't work that way. Sanctification is a life-long journey. Not until our last breath will the process end.

If we're honest, life often looks more like the childhood

game Chutes and Ladders than it does a straightforward race to a finish line. We take a few confident steps forward and then plummet down an unsuspecting chute. We often begin the day determined to live for Him and end it in discouragement over our shortcomings.

We might identify with Paul, who wrote:

> *For I know that nothing good dwells in me, that is, in my flesh. For I have the desire to do what is right, but not the ability to carry it out. For I do not do the good I want, but the evil I do not want is what I keep on doing. Now if I do what I do not want, it is no longer I who do it, but sin that dwells within me.*
> ROMANS 7:18–20 ESV

Without the grace of God, our lives would be bleak and frustrating, and we might even want to throw in the towel on the Christian life entirely. So how do we live without the unbearable discouragement that accompanies the realities of our human condition?

We remember who we are in light of all God has done for us. We recognize that He alone can break the cycle of sin in our lives and put us on the path to greater godliness. In the words of the great hymn writer, Charles Wesley:

> *He breaks the power of canceled sin,*
> *He sets the prisoner free;*

His blood can make the foulest clean,
His blood availed for me.[4]

We must pray to the God who breaks the power of canceled sin, and we must ask Him to do for us what we cannot do for ourselves. God longs to put the glory of His redeeming work on display in our lives. He takes sinful human beings and makes them sons and daughters.

If God is committed to our growth, so we should be. We should pray for each other that we would "walk in a manner worthy of the Lord, fully pleasing to him, bearing fruit in every good work and increasing in the knowledge of God" (Colossians 1:10 ESV).

Not to try our best every day because we are afraid of failure would be a worse sin than trying and failing on the path to greater growth.

Thankfully, God remains more committed to our sanctification in this life than we will ever be.

So, whether you eat or drink,
or whatever you do, do all to the glory of God.
1 CORINTHIANS 10:31 ESV

39.

FORGET IT

I consider that a man's brain originally is like a little empty attic, and you have to stock it with such furniture as you choose. . . . The skillful workman is very careful indeed as to what he takes into his brain-attic.

A Study in Scarlet

A Study in Scarlet contains one of the strangest and most widely discussed conversations in the canon. Watson is talking to Holmes about the fact that the earth revolves around the sun when suddenly the mastermind detective bursts:

> *"What the deuce is it to me?" he interrupted impatiently: "You say that we go round the sun. If we went round the moon it would not make a pennyworth of difference to me or to my work."*[1]

Holmes then vows to forget the scientific fact entirely since it might get in the way of truly useful information.

That Holmes does not know the Copernican theory is a strange admission from a man who prides himself on his scientific study. Holmes often references astronomy in his adventures, and yet he claims not to know such a fundamental fact. Even children in grade school understand that the earth revolves around the sun. How could an acclaimed scientist be so ignorant?

Holmes answered this question himself, saying: "I consider that a man's brain originally is like a little empty attic, and you have to stock it with such furniture as you choose."[2] Holmes didn't believe the brain was *like* an attic; he believed the brain *was* an attic—a finite space for storing valuable information. And he believed each person is responsible for stocking the attic with what he or she believes will be useful to life. Once the space is gone, no room is left for new or more valuable information.

As it turns out, Holmes' notion of a brain-attic is not such a bad concept. Scientific research on memory formation, retention, and retrieval seems to support the idea that we can only retain so many facts. Studies reveal that many of us try to do or remember too much at a time and fail to accomplish anything at all.

One of the great culprits in this regard is multitasking.

God the Creator understands how we as humans think. Perhaps this is why He simplified His expectations for us: "For the whole law is fulfilled in one word: 'You shall love your neighbor as yourself'" (Galatians 5:14 ESV). As His children, we are expected to stock our brain-attics with the truth of God's Word. Loving our neighbor as ourselves is mandatory because loving our neighbor is proof that we love our Father.

It is powerfully important to God that His children reach a lost world with the love of the Savior. One of the last things Christ said to His disciples before He went home to His Father was:

> *"All authority has been given to Me in heaven and on earth. Go therefore and make disciples of all the nations, baptizing them in the name of the Father and the Son and the Holy Spirit, teaching them to observe all that I commanded you; and lo, I am with you always, even to the end of the age."*
> MATTHEW 28:18–20 NASB

Jesus could have said anything. The stage was set. His followers clung to every sentence. No doubt the eleven disciples watched and listened with mixed emotions to the final words of the One they loved supremely. And what did Jesus choose to talk about?—showing love to other people.

The Great Commission is proof for us that nobody exists outside the boundary of our neighbor. We should strive to take the Gospel to every corner of the world—telling people about Christ so that they have the opportunity to spend eternity with Him.

Loving our neighbor is the fruit of genuine salvation and obedience to God. After loving God, loving our neighbor is the most important thing.

> *"And you shall love the Lord your God with all your*

heart and with all your soul and with all your mind
and with all your strength.' The second is this: 'You
shall love your neighbor as yourself.' There is no other
commandment greater than these"
MARK 12:30–31 ESV

As Christians, we have many ministries within the church that we can choose or not choose to participate in. We aren't required to sing in the choir, for instance, or to teach Sunday school, or to drive a bus. Fellow church members may ask us to do these things depending on the need and the gifts God has given us, but God's Word doesn't mandate that we all learn to play the piano or decide to preach. Love, however, is something else entirely.

Loving our neighbor is not an optional ministry.

"A new commandment I give to you,
that you love one another: just as I have
loved you, you also are to love one another."
JOHN 13:34 ESV

40.

GENUINE LIES

"What you do in this world is a matter of
no consequence. The question is, what can you
make people believe that you have done?"
A STUDY IN SCARLET

All is not as it seems.

When Conan Doyle set out to create Sherlock Holmes, he had no idea he was creating a model for the new detective or that he was writing the manual for criminal justice and crime solving. Had he known how carefully his manuscripts would be dissected in London and around the world for centuries after they were published, he might have reviewed each word in every entry a little closer.

The little things, after all, make the biggest difference.

"The Speckled Band" remains one of the most beloved stories in Arthur Conan Doyle's canon. The story includes an evil doctor who trains a deadly snake to climb a bellpull at the sound of a whistle. The snake is then rewarded with milk.

The only problems? Snakes don't hear sound, and they don't drink milk.

Still, fans have loved the story for decades, proving the point that what people believe is true can be as powerful as what is actually true.

Political advertisements are another example of this phenomenon. How often has a politician looked at the camera lens in earnest and made a list of promises—lower taxes, improved wages, increased jobs, reduced debt—only to take office and forget the promises were ever made? Yet people will return to the polls year after year and make decisions based on promises they want to believe.

We can laugh about the discrepancies as they pertain to Conan Doyle's stories or the politicians on Capitol Hill, but what we believe about God and His Word is an entirely different and altogether more critical matter. When it comes to the realities of God, what is true matters infinitely more than what anyone believes is true.

No doubt many readers of Holmes complete "The Speckled Band" without any inkling that the doctor could never have trained the snake to respond to a bell or to accept milk as a reward. These readers close their books and go on with their lives none the wiser. And really, the consequence of this oversight is not severe. Whether or not snakes drink milk has little bearing on everyday life.

How many Christians hear half-truths about God or misconceptions about His Word and respond in the same way as their "Speckled Band" counterparts?

The consequence of this oversight can be deadly.

We should heed the children's song that says:

O be careful little ears what you hear
O be careful little ears what you hear
For the Father up above
Is looking down in love,
So, be careful little ears what you hear.

Simple but profound.

Discernment is a nonnegotiable in the Christian life if we wish to be stable in our faith and not be tossed around by every wind of doctrine. The world and even halfhearted Christians wish to bombard us with false truths about God.

In Luke 8, Jesus tells the parable of the lamp under the jar:

> *"No one after lighting a lamp covers it with a jar*
> *or puts it under a bed, but puts it on a stand, so that*
> *those who enter may see the light. For nothing is hidden*
> *that will not be made manifest, nor is anything secret*
> *that will not be known and come to light."*
> LUKE 8:16–17 ESV

He then says something very interesting in the verse immediately following: "Take care then how you hear" (Luke 8:18 ESV).Where we might have expected Him to say, "Take care what you do" or "Take care how you look," instead we see, "Take care how you hear."

It would seem that Jesus is linking our testimony to our

discernment, both because of what shapes our thinking as well as what we then turn around and communicate to others about the God we serve.

As believers, we should be so informed by our personal study of God's Word that we emphatically and systematically reject any suggestion about God that is not true or does not conform to His Word. We must be so dedicated to having discerning ears that we follow the nudge in our spirit to check things out—as opposed to simply ignoring or accepting them—when they raise flags of doubt in our mind. " 'God is spirit, and those who worship him must worship in spirit and truth'" (John 4:24 ESV).

What we believe about God is the most important thing we will ever believe, but what is true about God matters infinitely more than what we believe is true about God.

The sum of your word is truth, and every one of your righteous rules endures forever.
PSALM 119:160 ESV

41.

THE NOT-SO-HUMBLE HOLMES

*"The chief proof of man's real greatness lies
in his perception of his own smallness."*
THE SIGN OF FOUR

Sherlock Holmes craved personal recognition. In "The Adventure of the Greek Interpreter" he said: "I cannot agree with those who rank modesty among the virtues."[1]

Dr. Watson liked to say that Holmes responded to the positive attention of his many adoring fans the same way girls do when someone comments on their beauty. What might this reaction include? The false modesty, the blush of approval, or the strut of awareness. Holmes was anything but meek.

The opposite of *humble* is *Holmes*. So, too, sometimes the opposite of *Christian* is *humble*.

In 1988, a philosopher named Dallas Willard wrote of Christianity:

*One of the greatest fallacies of our faith, and actually
one of the greatest acts of unbelief, is the thought that
our spiritual acts and virtues need to be advertised to be
known. The frantic efforts of religious personages and*

groups to advertise and certify themselves is a stunning
revelation of their lack of substance and faith.[2]

Willard makes a good point. Even in the church—where we are taught to be humble—we can be tempted to prove our worth to Christ and His people by drawing attention to the exercise of our own gifts. We want people to know what we are doing for God, as if being seen by men is the key to being approved by God.

Or maybe, if we're honest with ourselves, we aren't even doing the good deeds for God.

Consider the jobs in the church that are most quickly filled versus those that require hours on end of creative recruiting. Leadership, teaching, and music opportunities generally fill faster than nursery, cleaning, or maintenance jobs. Often, the same people who are quick to take the microphone are slow to do other, less public ministry.

Who wants to manage the bus route or lock up the church building? Little thanks is given to the woman who sanitizes the toys in the toddler room on Saturday mornings. How many feelings get hurt when one soloist is selected from a group of worthy participants? Certainly more feelings than are hurt when someone else is selected to visit the shut-ins or clean out the closets in the church gym. Church fundraisers are often most successful when people can opt to put their names on tiny brass plates in the expansive church lobby for everyone to see.

This is human nature.

We must ask ourselves why we do the things we do. The Bible provides us with a clear expectation: "Be completely humble and gentle; be patient, bearing with one another in love" (Ephesians 4:2 NIV).

If we are doing things for God, why is it important that anyone else know? This doesn't mean we refuse the leadership role, cease from teaching, or disengage from opportunities to minister in music. God has graciously given all of these gifts, and each of these roles is important. To neglect using a gift is another sin entirely. We must be good stewards of every occasion God gives us to serve.

But we should diligently and ruthlessly question our motives at every opportunity. Jealousy, frustration, or unkindness with someone else who is exercising a public gift is a symptom that we are not ministering for God. "Whatever you do, work heartily, as for the Lord and not for men, knowing that from the Lord you will receive the inheritance as your reward. You are serving the Lord Christ" (Colossians 3:23–24 ESV).

Despite what we sometimes believe, humility doesn't happen as a result of being engrossed with our flaws. Deflecting praise by listing personal weaknesses is not humility. Andrew Murray, a pastor and contemporary of Conan Doyle, wrote: "Not to be occupied with your sin, but to be occupied with God brings deliverance from self."[3]

Humility, then, is *more of God and less of me.*

When we arrive at the realization that everything we do is for an audience of One, humility will be the natural byproduct. We will serve Him without care or concern for the admiration of others. We won't mind when we are overlooked for one opportunity to serve because we know we will find another place in which to invest our time and resources. We will recognize that receiving an opportunity to serve and not receiving an opportunity to serve come equally from the hand of God.

One solution to the pride problem is to do good things secretly. Nothing speaks of the love of Christ like good deeds done anonymously. An envelope of cash given to someone with a financial need or a typed letter of encouragement tucked in the pastor's office box speaks volumes to the recipient. When our name isn't the focal point of something we intend to give someone else, the recipient is free to focus on the Great Giver—Jesus Christ.

Long after life as we know it has ceased and our work on earth is done, we will celebrate for all eternity each cup of cold water given in God's name.

Therefore humble yourselves under the mighty hand of God, that He may exalt you at the proper time.
1 PETER 5:6 NASB

42.

THE SINCEREST FORM OF FLATTERY

*"I have frequently gained my first real insight into
the character of parents by studying their children."*
THE ADVENTURE OF THE COPPER BEECHES

Every artist has a muse. For Arthur Conan Doyle, his inspiration for Sherlock Holmes came from his professor and mentor, Dr. Joseph Bell, whom he learned from in medical school. Dr. Bell is credited for pioneering the concept of deduction. He was able to make medical diagnoses based on close observation alone. Conan Doyle once explained, "He would look at the patient—he would hardly allow the patient to open his mouth—but he would make his diagnosis of the disease entirely by his part of observation."[1]

To further prove his skill, Bell often selected a stranger from a crowd, observed him, and determined the person's occupation and recent activities based upon scrutiny alone.

Sound familiar?

Doyle watched his mentor do this so often that it sparked an idea that led to the creation of Sherlock Holmes, and the rest is history.

Dr. Bell was aware of Conan Doyle's writing and took pride in being the inspiration behind Sherlock Holmes.

Bell once accused Conan Doyle, "You are yourself Sherlock Holmes and well you know it."[2] He was right, of course, though Doyle wasn't quick to admit it. At least twice in Doyle's lifetime, the author participated in criminal investigations of free men who had been wrongfully convicted. How did he do it? He used the methods of his character, Sherlock Holmes, of course!

In "The Adventure of the Copper Beeches" Holmes is explaining to Watson that—just as a doctor could look to a child's genetic medical history to explain an odd illness—so, too, deductions about an adult's moral character could be inferred from his or her child's behavior. Holmes and Watson were discussing a specific child in question when Holmes said:

> *"This child's disposition is abnormally cruel, merely*
> *for cruelty's sake, and whether he derives this from his*
> *smiling father, as I should suspect, or from his mother,*
> *it bodes evil for the poor girl who is in their power."[3]*

How sad that a distressed child would indicate an evil parent. And yet Holmes was on to something important when he drew this conclusion.

It has been said a hundred different ways that imitation is the sincerest form of flattery. Doyle, himself, is an example of this. One of the greatest compliments to his writing is the number of instances in which he has been parodied over the course of a century. Mark Twain and A. A. Milne are among the more notorious authors who imitated Doyle, but many lesser-known authors have done the same. Followers imitate the people they most want to emulate.

So, too, we as Christians must learn to imitate Christ. The principle evidence of saving faith is Christlikeness. "Whoever claims to live in him must live as Jesus did" (1 John 2:6 NIV).

To be a Christian, in the truest sense of the word, is more than praying a prayer or subscribing to a belief system. It is more than sitting in a pew or tithing to a church. Though these tasks are important evidences of belonging to God, being a Christian literally means *learning Christ*.

What is a Christian? Charles Hodge, a well-regarded theologian who lived at the same time as Conan Doyle answered it this way: "It is being so constrained by a sense of the love of our divine Lord to us, that we consecrate our lives to him."[4]

The significance of belonging to God, then, is that our greatest motivation for obeying Him comes out of our love for Him as opposed to our guilt. We should want to be like Christ because we love God, not because we are scared of hell.

Being motivated by love instead of guilt may not feel like it should make that much of a difference—especially if the resulting behavior looks the same—but in reality, motive changes everything. Consider this. If someone threatened to harm a beloved member of your family, would you defend your family member out of duty or love? And if so, how would it change the circumstance?

Duty motivates us to meet the requirements; love motivates us to give all that we have.

The truth is, sin poses the greatest threat to our relationship with God. When love of God becomes our chief motivation for obedience, we will sin less. Our love for Christ should be so evident that unbelievers can arrive at correct conclusions about God based on observing our lives. How unbelievably sad it would be for a child of God to do something that would disparage our heavenly Father.

So what does imitating Christ look like? The Bible is filled with commentary on the character of Christ. We know that our standard of righteousness is the character of God. A good place to start is in the Psalms. "The LORD is gracious and merciful, slow to anger and abounding in steadfast love. The LORD is good to all, and his mercy is over all that he has made" (Psalm 145:8–9 ESV).

Many fathers have sent their children out the door for the evening with the reminder of who they are and whom they represent. "Remember, you are a Smith!" a dad might say, or, "Don't forget! You are a Jones!" The same is true for us.

Remember, you belong to God!

> *Imitate God, therefore, in everything you do,*
> *because you are his dear children.*
> EPHESIANS 5:1 NLT

43

A MATTER OF PERSPECTIVE

*"God help us! Why does fate play such
tricks with poor, helpless worms?"*
THE BOSCOMBE VALLEY MYSTERY

More often than not, Sherlock Holmes demonstrated how *not* to conduct a healthy personal life. Throughout his adventures, he taught us how *not* to make friends, how *not* to treat women, how *not* to interact with family, how *not* to talk to children, how *not* to respond to victory, and how *not* to maintain a house. The list could go on.

He is a fascinating and unreasonable enigma—an oddball who is as good at detection as he is bad at life. Still, Sherlock Holmes remains a favorite character for many readers and fans. Why?

The person telling the story makes all the difference.

In the case of the canon, Dr. Watson narrated all but four of the sixty stories. Two are narrated by Sherlock Holmes, and two are narrated by an ambiguous storyteller. Fortunately for the great detective, Watson was a friend and fan of Sherlock Holmes, otherwise the stories might have read very differently.

We might describe Sherlock Holmes as a bony, narcissistic,

demanding detective with ink on his hands and bullet holes in his walls. Dr. Watson described him this way:

> *In height he was rather over six feet, and so excessively lean that he seemed to be considerably taller. His eyes were sharp and piercing, save during those intervals of torpor to which I have alluded; and his thin, hawk-like nose gave his whole expression an air of alertness and decision. His chin, too, had the prominence and squareness which mark the man of determination. His hands were invariably blotted with ink and stained with chemicals, yet he was possessed of extraordinary delicacy of touch, as I frequently had occasion to observe when I watched him manipulating his fragile philosophical instruments.[1]*

In other words, he who narrates the story controls the perspective. As children of God, we know this to be true of our own life.

Consider your own story. When you look at the details of your life, what do you see? An imperfect appearance, a talentless church member, or a deficient friend? Maybe you see a sea of past mistakes or an ocean of missed opportunities.

If you are comparing yourself to someone else, then maybe you are right to make these deductions. View your life from the vantage point of God, however, and you will see something else entirely.

Blessed be the God and Father of our Lord Jesus Christ,
who has blessed us in Christ with every spiritual
blessing in the heavenly places, even as he chose us in
him before the foundation of the world, that we should
be holy and blameless before him. In love he predestined
us for adoption as sons through Jesus Christ, according to
the purpose of his will, to the praise of his glorious grace,
with which he has blessed us in the Beloved.
EPHESIANS 1:3–6 ESV

Before Jesus came to earth—or redemption's story unfolded—God chose you. Let that sink into the deep waters of your heart. He formed you in your mother's womb, removed the grip of death on your soul, and adopted you into His family if you know Him as your Savior.

God is the great narrator of your story. Every deviation from a path you would have chosen is a detour for good and not for evil.

From the creation of the world, Genesis 1—"In the beginning, God"—to the end of the age, Revelation 22—"Surely I am coming soon"—God is telling the story. He knows the beginning of the story and the end. He *is* the beginning and the end of the story. He has a wholly different perspective, and we should be eternally grateful. If we were in charge of the story, it would read differently.

> *Your eyes saw my unformed substance; in your book*
> *were written, every one of them, the days that were*
> *formed for me, when as yet there was none of them.*
> *How precious to me are your thoughts, O God!*
> *How vast is the sum of them!*
> PSALM 139:16–17 ESV

We need only trust Him. Dissatisfaction or worry over the details of our story displays distrust in the sovereignty of God. God does not abandon the work of His hands. "'Look at the birds of the air: they neither sow nor reap nor gather into barns, and yet your heavenly Father feeds them. Are you not of more value than they?'" (Matthew 6:26 ESV).

God is carefully managing the details of our lives—*all of them*. He knows everything from who will be the next president to how long the sparrows will live.

And perhaps most remarkably, both are of significance to Him.

> *For it is God who is at work in you,*
> *both to will and to work for His good pleasure.*
> PHILIPPIANS 2:13 NASB

44.
CRIME FILES

*"My mind is like a racing engine, tearing itself
to pieces because it is not connected up
with the work for which it was built."*
THE ADVENTURE OF WISTERIA LODGE

Two hundred sixty-three bodies. One hundred nineteen murders.

The canon is full of mysteries and manslaughter, celebrating the one person who can handle the mess with the calm intelligence befitting his profession: Sherlock Holmes.

Today—one hundred years after the book was closed on the adventures of Holmes and Watson—221B Baker Street still receives letters from anxious wannabe clients, claiming wrongful accusations and begging the great detective to get involved in their case.

Sherlock Holmes was so successful solving crimes, murder or otherwise, that people often asked to hire his creator, Arthur Conan Doyle, to solve their real-life mysteries. By the end of Doyle's life, he was a much-sought-after crime consultant.

In the early twentieth century, for example, twenty-seven-year-old George Edalji wrote a letter—not to Sherlock

Holmes, but to Arthur Conan Doyle—asking for help. Edalji served three years hard labor after being convicted on a charge of injuring a pony. He was eventually pardoned after Arthur Conan Doyle led a campaign to overturn his conviction.

Can you imagine reaching out to one of today's notorious crime writers and asking him or her to solve your real-life case? Most of us wouldn't even consider it. This is yet another example of how the line between fact and fiction became blurred in the world of the mastermind detective.

T. S. Eliot was a fellow writer and contemporary of Conan Doyle. He was also a fan of Sherlock Holmes. He once said: "Perhaps the greatest of the Sherlock Holmes mysteries is this: that when we talk of him we invariably fall into the fantasy of his existence."[1]

Unfortunately for fans of Holmes, Conan Doyle was not the real deal when it came to detective work, and in time it became clear that he was a writer and not made for the world of crime solving. He eventually hung up his investigative hat and returned to his chief ambitions.

So, too, our identity as children of God should indicate we were not made for this world. It is easy to get caught up in the daily responsibilities of life on earth. We have friends and family, jobs and community, church and school—and we should be invested in these outlets, doing our best as unto the Lord. We were put on this earth for a reason. But we should also remember that this life is not all there is for us—not even close. This world is not our home.

C. S. Lewis, a contemporary of Conan Doyle, wrote in his book *Mere Christianity*: "If I find in myself a desire which no experience in this world can satisfy, the most probable explanation is that I was made for another world."[2]

This pilgrim mentality was not unique to Lewis. The Bible spoke of it long before Lewis did. Hebrews 11 says of faithful men and women:

> *These all died in faith, not having received the things promised, but having seen them and greeted them from afar, and having acknowledged that they were strangers and exiles on the earth. For people who speak thus make it clear that they are seeking a homeland.*
> HEBREWS 11:13–14 ESV

Conan Doyle was a brilliant author—smart enough that he could play the role of a true-life detective successfully for a while—but he was not made for crime solving. He was made to write about it.

As pilgrims on earth, we should strive never to become too comfortable in our environment. We should hold the gifts of this life with open hands, and we should be sure the enjoyment of God is our chief ambition. We may be able to play the role of citizen on earth for a while, but we as the children of God were not made for earth living.

We were made for heaven and the eternal presence of God.

We should be able to say with the preacher, Jonathan Edwards:

To go to heaven, fully to enjoy God, is infinitely better than the most pleasant accommodations here. Better than fathers and mothers, husbands, wives, or children, or the company of any, or all earthly friends. These are but shadows; but the enjoyment of God is the substance. These are but scattered beams; but God is the sun. These are but streams; but God is the fountain. These are but drops, but God is the ocean.[3]

We are "looking for the city which has foundations, whose architect and builder is God" (Hebrews 11:10 NASB).

So in the meantime, let's live like travelers.

But we are citizens of heaven, where the Lord Jesus Christ lives. And we are eagerly waiting for him to return as our Savior.
PHILIPPIANS 3:20 NLT

45

MIND OVER MATTER

"You did not know where to look,
and so you missed all that was important."
A Case of Identity

Sherlock Holmes was continually astounded by the ignorance of the Scotland Yard inspectors. And, consistent with his style, Holmes never remained quiet about it. He wasted no time criticizing the police as he leveled his first insult in the first story, *A Study in Scarlet*:

> *"It is indeed kind of you to come," [Officer Gregson] said,*
> *"I have had everything left untouched."*
> *"Except that!" [Sherlock Holmes] answered,*
> *pointing at the pathway. "If a herd of buffaloes had*
> *passed along there could not be a greater mess. No doubt,*
> *however, you had drawn your own conclusions, Gregson,*
> *before you permitted this."[1]*

And so the less-than-amicable partnership between Sherlock Holmes and Scotland Yard began.

During one particular conversation in *The Valley of Fear*

in which Holmes and an inspector were discussing the name *Jonathan Wild*, the inspector said he thought he recognized the name as having been a character in a detective novel. Holmes responded:

> *"Jonathan Wild wasn't a detective, and he wasn't in a novel. He was a master criminal, and he lived last century—1750 or thereabouts."*
>
> *"Then he's no use to me. I'm a practical man," [said the inspector].*
>
> *"Mr. Mac, the most practical thing that you ever did in your life would be to shut yourself up for three months and read twelve hours a day at the annals of crime."*[2]

This was Sherlock Holmes' way of saying to the inspector, "Do your homework!"

The tension between Sherlock Holmes and the London police is well documented in the canon. Scotland Yard appears in forty-two of the sixty stories. Holmes' biggest complaint is that the inspectors do not know how to think properly about crime. His advice to the inspector to spend three months studying criminal history for twelve hours a day is good counsel. Roughly 1100 hours studying any subject would be beneficial to someone in need of educating.

So it is true for the Christian. What would happen if we spent even a fraction of 1100 hours over the course of three months studying the Word of God? Change would be almost certain. How could we study God's Word so thoroughly and not come away wiser? No doubt we would finish our study with a radically improved view of God, sin, and self.

A. W. Tozer was an American pastor, author, and magazine editor who lived at the same time as Conan Doyle. In his book *The Knowledge of the Holy*, Tozer begins the first chapter with these words: "What comes into our minds when we think about God is the most important thing about us."[3] He was right, of course. We think of a thousand things over the course of a day, but nothing is as important as what we think of our Creator.

The Old Testament bears record of the benefit of thinking about God: "You keep him in perfect peace whose mind is stayed on you, because he trusts in you" (Isaiah 26:3 ESV). The New Testament tells us that loving God involves the way we think: "And he said to him, 'You shall love the Lord your God with all your heart and with all your soul and with all your mind'" (Matthew 22:37 ESV). But this type of thinking is not accidental or involuntary.

Sherlock Holmes was right to imply correct thinking doesn't *just happen*. Thinking correctly is a direct result of studying the right things—of applying ourselves to the knowledge that will inform our understanding.

In the New Testament, John recorded his gospel because he desperately wanted people to believe in Jesus Christ. He records an interesting conversation Jesus had with the people of God: "So Jesus said to the Jews who had believed him, 'If you abide in my word, you are truly my disciples, and you will know the truth, and the truth will set you free'" (John 8:31–32 ESV). This verse—and scores of others like it—seems to imply that studying leads to knowledge, and knowledge leads to freedom. Our thinking informs our behavior.

One of the reasons studying the Bible is so important for the child of God is because our own thoughts inform our behavior more than the external babble of anyone else. We listen to ourselves more than we listen to anybody else. So it is critical that our thoughts be informed by the truth of God.

We would do well to shut ourselves up for three months and read our Bibles for twelve hours a day. Since that is impossible for most of us, given the speed and responsibilities of life, we should at least commit ourselves to spend a few precious minutes every day reading the Word of God and applying it to life.

In short, right thinking produces right action.

> *Finally, brothers, whatever is true, whatever is*
> *honorable, whatever is just, whatever is pure,*
> *whatever is lovely, whatever is commendable,*
> *if there is any excellence, if there is anything*
> *worthy of praise, think about these things.*
> PHILIPPIANS 4:8 ESV

46.

A NOTE ON MUSIC

*"There is nothing more to be said or to be done tonight,
so hand me over my violin and let us try to forget
for half an hour the miserable weather and the
still more miserable ways of our fellowmen."*
THE FIVE ORANGE PIPS

Sherlock Holmes is most universally recognized with the help of three objects. First, he is known for his deerstalker cap—the hat with the wide brim, side flaps, and top tie. Sidney Paget was the original illustrator of Arthur Conan Doyle's stories, and it was Paget—not Conan Doyle—who decided to draw a deerstalker cap on the head of the famous detective. Doyle never referenced the hat in any of his stories, yet it has been on Holmes' head ever since.

Second, Holmes is known for his calabash pipe—the big yellow pipe with the white top. In the sixty stories featuring the great detective, only four do not reference him smoking. If the printed stories of Sherlock Holmes could be scratch-and-sniff, they would surely reek of tobacco. The calabash pipe, however, is another of the items never found in the canon. An actor named William Gillette played the role of the great detective in the late nineteenth and early twentieth century and used a calabash pipe. Thus the image has remained.

Finally, Sherlock Holmes is frequently associated with the violin. This object, unlike the other two, is consistent with the canon. The fact that Holmes loves playing the violin and enjoys attending concerts is true to the vision and writing of Conan Doyle.

One of the first questions Holmes ever posed to Dr. Watson when determining if they would be compatible roommates was whether or not he minded the violin. "It depends on the player," answers Watson. "A well-played violin is a treat for the gods—a badly played one—."[1] And with those words, the violin became a sort of supporting character throughout the canon, a fixture appearing often and in the least expected places.

In "The Adventure of the Mazarin Stone," for example, Dr. Watson finds himself in the untidy room of the first floor in Baker Street. "He looked round him at the scientific charts upon the wall, the acid-charred bench of chemicals, the violin-case leaning in the corner."[2] In "The Adventure of the Cardboard Box," Dr. Watson recounts having: "a pleasant little meal together, during which Holmes would talk about nothing but violins, narrating with great exultation how he had purchased his own Stradivarius."[3]

Sherlock Holmes is fiction's most famous violinist.

With all his eccentricities and weaknesses of character, the fact that Holmes loved music helped redeem him on the page. Readers unknowingly ask themselves, *How bad could this guy be if he appreciates the beauty of the violin?*

In truth, music changes people. Music is one of the greatest gifts God gave the human race. God's people have passed down psalms, hymns, and spiritual songs from generation to generation, setting to beautiful tunes the testimonies of God's goodness. Believers have used music to communicate the Gospel for centuries. The Bible includes more than four hundred references to singing and at least fifty times commands Christians to sing.

And yet music remains one of the most controversial subjects in the church. Everyone, it seems, has an opinion about *what* should be sung and *how*. Congregations are formed and split over musical choices. Passionate arguments ensue in seminary classrooms and at kitchen tables. All of this can only indicate one thing: music is a powerful tool in the body of Christ. When God's people sing together, they demonstrate more clearly than at any other time the unity of mind and mouth that God longs to see in His people. Music shapes what we think, what we desire, and what we pursue.

Jonathan Edwards, a preacher who lived one hundred years before Conan Doyle, once wrote:

> *The best, most beautiful, and most perfect way that we have of expressing a sweet concord of mind to each other,*

is by music. When I would form in my mind an idea of
a society in the highest degree happy, I think of them as
expressing their love, their joy, and the inward concord
and harmony and spiritual beauty of their souls by
sweetly singing to each other.[4]

This view of music should cause us to stop and evaluate our own perspective. Do we think of music as simply a filler of time before the preaching? Do we really think about what we are singing, or do we use the music service to mentally check through a personal to-do list or review conversations from earlier in the day? Do we consider the ways music can encourage our brothers and sisters in the service? Do we understand that our music communicates what we believe to be true about God?

The Bible indicates a link between what we sing and how we live: "My heart is steadfast, O God, my heart is steadfast; I will sing, yes, I will sing praises!" (Psalm 57:7 NASB).

God was kind to give us music, and we should be eager to use it to honor Him.

Let the word of Christ dwell in you richly,
teaching and admonishing one another in all
wisdom, singing psalms and hymns and spiritual
songs, with thankfulness in your hearts to God.
Colossians 3:16 esv

WORK IT OUT

"My mind," he said, "rebels at stagnation.
Give me problems, give me work, give me the most
abstruse cryptogram or the most intricate analysis,
and I am in my own proper atmosphere."
THE SIGN OF FOUR

The only thing scarier than Sherlock Holmes being wrong is Sherlock Holmes being bored. Being without a case to solve was known to put Sherlock Holmes in a bad mood. And according to Dr. Watson, Holmes was often disgruntled. When this happened, "[Holmes] would sit in an arm-chair, with his hair-trigger and a hundred Boxer cartridges, and proceed to adorn the opposite wall with a patriotic V.R. done in bullet-pocks."[1] Side note: "V.R." stands for Victoria Regina, the royal monogram of the Queen Victoria who reigned when Sherlock Holmes was alive and working.

Taken at face value, Holmes' habit of shooting at his wall is disturbing. If someone today decided to fill a wall of his house with bullets, he would likely end up behind bars or in a psychiatric ward. Shooting the wall is typically a bad idea.

Holmes made no secret of needing something to occupy his mind. In Conan Doyle's second novel, *The Sign of Four*,

Holmes says, "I abhor the dull routine of existence. I crave for mental exaltation."[2] By his own admission, Sherlock Holmes dabbled in drugs as a direct result of being bored.

Boredom rarely results in good decisions either for the great detective or for us. Though boredom is not itself a sin, it can lead us to make poor choices. "Go to the ant, O sluggard, Observe her ways and be wise" (Proverbs 6:6 NASB). God created a way of escape for boredom: He created work.

It is a misunderstanding of scripture to believe that work is a result of the curse. While work certainly became more difficult—as did all aspects of living in a fallen world—work was created and enjoyed prior to Adam's sin. Before the fall of man: "The LORD God took the man and put him in the garden of Eden to work it and keep it" (Genesis 2:15 ESV).

God Himself worked when He created the world, and He is certainly not living under the curse of sin. He demonstrated how He desires we busy ourselves as His children—wholeheartedly, creatively, and excellently—for His glory. Nowhere does God instruct us to do aimless, mindless, or useless work. Neither does He instruct us to work for the praise of men. He calls us to take on tasks that will glorify Him, and He equips us with gifts, interests, and abilities unique to us so that we can accomplish the work He calls us to do. Better still, He rewards us with peace and satisfaction when we work. "Sweet is the sleep of a laborer" (Ecclesiastes 5:12 ESV). God created human beings to work. Therefore, we are most fulfilled when we obey God and work hard. God gave us work as a gift. To believe otherwise is to accept a lie.

An unsuspecting nugget of truth exists in Arthur Conan Doyle's "The Adventure of the Empty House." Sherlock Holmes, talking to Dr. Watson, says: "Work is the best antidote to sorrow, my dear Watson."[3] Anyone who has been given a task during moments of deep grief understands that work can be a gift on life's darkest days.

Any work that is done for God is not done in vain. To this end, we must be sure we do the right things for the right reason. We must work for the glory of God—more than the approval of a boss or the pat on the back from a superior—giving our utmost care that nothing about our work detracts from God's glory.

T. S. Eliot, a contemporary of Arthur Conan Doyle and a fan of Sherlock Holmes, wrote:

The last temptation is the greatest treason: To do the right deed for the wrong reason.[4]

Many of God's children have gone into the workforce and climbed the corporate ladder without so much as a nod to the glory of God. This isn't His desire. It isn't enough to work hard or work well. We must work for Him.

We must strive every day to allow His glory to control our choices and govern our work. Our starting place in every decision must be His glory and not our own. In the words of Paul: "Therefore, my beloved brothers, be steadfast, immovable, always abounding in the work of the Lord, knowing that in the Lord your labor is not in vain" (1 Corinthians 15:58 ESV).

Work provides us with tangible opportunities to make His glory known. As long as there is work to be done, no child of God has an excuse to be bored.

Whatever you do, work at it with all your heart,
as working for the Lord, not for human masters.
COLOSSIANS 3:23 NIV

48

THE GREATEST GAME

Come, Watson, come! The game is afoot.
Not a word! Into your clothes and come!
THE ADVENTURE OF THE ABBEY GRANGE

An entire book could be compiled using only the best quotes in the canon. One quote to be included was uttered by Sherlock Holmes to Dr. Watson in "The Adventure of the Abbey Grange": "Come, Watson, come! The game is afoot. Not a word! Into your clothes and come!"[1] This is one of the most famous quotes uttered by the great detective. It was borrowed from Shakespeare. Conan Doyle loved giving subtle (and sometimes not-so-subtle) nods to the writers who most influenced his own work.

This particular quote was first spoken in Shakespeare's *Henry V*, Act 3, Scene 1. Shakespeare's play is based on the events surrounding the Battle of Agincourt during the Hundred Years' War. King Henry, in an effort to rouse the troops, cries:

I see you stand like greyhounds in the slips,
Straining upon the start. The game's afoot:
Follow your spirit, and upon this charge

Cry 'God for Harry, England, and Saint George!'[2]

So, too, Holmes decided to rouse a sleeping Dr. Watson with the same invitation.

> *It was on a bitterly cold and frosty morning, towards the end of the winter of '97, that I was awakened by a tugging at my shoulder. It was Holmes. The candle in his hand shone upon his eager, stooping face, and told me at a glance that something was amiss.*
>
> *"Come, Watson, come!" he cried. "The game is afoot. Not a word! Into your clothes and come!"[3]*

It is important to understand that the phrase, "The game is afoot!" is not a reference to a sporting event like soccer or chess. "Game" in this case refers to the hunting of an animal.

Ten minutes after Holmes cries, "Come, Watson, come!" the pair is in a cab, rattling through the silent streets on their way to one of their most famous and intriguing adventures. They will arrive on the scene of a murder where Eustace Brackenstall has been killed, supposedly by burglars, and Holmes, no surprise, will throw the case wide open with new insights.

It all began with an abrupt call to action early in the morning. Dr. Watson, no doubt, was taken by surprise even though he knew Holmes well enough to understand that anything could happen at any time.

So, too, as believers, we watch and wait for the moment when the Lord will come like a thief in the night and take us on our most important journey yet. We cannot know the day or the hour, but we have been told to be ready. And we know God is always true to His Word.

But the day of the Lord will come like a thief, and then the heavens will pass away with a roar, and the heavenly bodies will be burned up and dissolved, and the earth and the works that are done on it will be exposed.
2 PETER 3:10 ESV

One of the most essential questions we should ask ourselves while we wait for the coming of the Lord is: *How do I endure until the end?* We face countless temptations and opportunities to fall away. Even the ordinary pleasures in this life distract us from the better thing.

Luke 17 talks about the coming of the kingdom and compares it to Noah's flood and Sodom and Gomorrah's destruction.

Just as it was in the days of Noah, so will it be in the days of the Son of Man. They were eating and drinking and marrying and being given in marriage, until the day when Noah entered the ark, and the flood came and

destroyed them all. Likewise, just as it was in the days
of Lot—they were eating and drinking, buying and
selling, planting and building, but on the day when
Lot went out from Sodom, fire and sulfur rained
from heaven and destroyed them all—so will it be
on the day when the Son of Man is revealed.
LUKE 17:26–30 ESV

No doubt, in the days of Noah and of Lot, many evil practices were taking place. Yet the Bible lists the following activities as distractions: eating, drinking, marrying, buying, selling, planting, and building. None of which are wrong in and of themselves. Neutral things that distract us from important things are not harmless things; they are hazardous things.

Consider the famous pair of sisters in scripture:

As Jesus and his disciples were on their way, he came to a
village where a woman named Martha opened her home
to him. She had a sister called Mary, who sat at the Lord's
feet listening to what he said. But Martha was distracted
by all the preparations that had to be made. She came to
him and asked, "Lord, don't you care that my sister has left
me to do the work by myself? Tell her to help me!"
"Martha, Martha," the Lord answered, "you are
worried and upset about many things, but few things
are needed—or indeed only one. Mary has chosen what

is better, and it will not be taken away from her."
LUKE 10:38–42 NIV

So often, like Martha, we are tempted to be distracted by the details of everyday life and miss the one needful thing.

If we really believed God was coming back tonight, what would we do differently? We ought to live our life in such a way that our answer would be a confident, "Nothing!"

Perseverance happens as a result of prayerfully prioritizing the events in daily life so as to keep God and His commands the main thing.

For you yourselves are fully aware that the day
of the Lord will come like a thief in the night.
1 THESSALONIANS 5:2 ESV

49.

INSIDE EVIL

"Avoid the moor in those hours of darkness
when the powers of evil are exalted."
THE HOUND OF THE BASKERVILLES

Sherlock Holmes and Professor Moriarty cannot be understood apart from each other. They exist to foil and frustrate each other's plans.

Throughout the adventures of Sherlock Holmes, Moriarty is responsible for helping nearly all of the criminals in London's underworld. He offers his assistance with a crime in exchange for a piece of the profit. This arrangement between Moriarty and a far-reaching band of lawbreakers comprises an intelligent criminal network.

Sherlock Holmes is determined to put an end to the work of Moriarty once and for all. At times, destroying Moriarty becomes more of an obsession than fighting for justice. Holmes' last words in "The Final Problem" before he battles Moriarty at Reichenbach Falls include:

"I am pleased to think that I shall be able to free society
from any further effects of [Moriarty's] presence, though
I fear that it is at a cost which will give pain to my
friends, and especially, my dear Watson, to you."[1]

Holmes' greatest goal is bringing down Moriarty's vast criminal empire, even if it costs him his life. To Sherlock Holmes, Moriarty represents all that is evil in the world.

Side note: As a child, Conan Doyle hated doing math at school, so it is no coincidence he made Moriarty a professor of mathematics.

The Hound of the Baskervilles begins with a friendly contest between Holmes and Watson. They are guessing the identity of the person who has left a walking stick at 221B Baker Street while waiting to speak to the great detective. Of no surprise, Holmes correctly guesses the man's identity just in time for Dr. Mortimer to return for his walking stick.

Dr. Mortimer wishes to talk to Holmes about the legendary "Curse of the Baskervilles." In chapter six of *The Hound of the Baskervilles*, Sherlock Holmes is talking to Sir Henry Baskerville when he says: "Avoid the moor in those hours of darkness when the powers of evil are exalted."[2] This is good advice. It is also biblical advice.

As believers, this quote should remind us of the many warnings throughout the book of Proverbs, a book overflowing with warnings to escape sin and temptation by avoiding the places where evil is practiced.

> *Do not enter the path of the wicked, and do not walk in the way of the evil. Avoid it; do not go on it; turn away from it and pass on. For they cannot sleep unless they*

have done wrong; they are robbed of sleep
unless they have made someone stumble.
PROVERBS 4:14–16 ESV

A few chapters later, Proverbs warns against going the way of the strange woman.

Let not your heart turn aside to her ways; do not stray
into her paths, for many a victim has she laid low, and
all her slain are a mighty throng. Her house is the way
to Sheol, going down to the chambers of death.
PROVERBS 7:25–27 ESV

It is worth noting that Proverbs doesn't say, "Don't be immoral." It says, "Don't go anywhere near the temptation." Another way to communicate Proverbs 7:25 would be: *Avoid the immoral woman's house in those hours of darkness when the powers of evil are exalted.*

Proverbs 7:25–27 could apply to life in other ways. *Avoid the Internet in those hours of darkness when the powers of evil are exalted. Avoid the circle of friends who are a bad influence in those hours of darkness when the powers of evil are exalted.* The list could go on.

It is crucial that we never think that we can handle any sin. Sin is strong and we are weak, and we are wise to remember it. A blatant disregard for the warnings we are given or an intentional stomping off toward the damp darkness of the moor—however "the moor" is represented in our life—is asking for destruction. So, too, is harboring positive *what-ifs* or creative fantasies about wrongdoing. "If I had cherished iniquity in my heart, the Lord would not have listened" (Psalm 66:18 ESV). To *cherish iniquity in our heart* is to maintain a positive disposition toward sin. It is to nourish a thing for which Christ died. It is to believe in ignorance that we are capable of flirting with destruction and surviving it. We must deal with even the trace evidence of sin in our lives immediately and relentlessly.

Thomas Watson was a Puritan preacher and author who lived more than two hundred years before Arthur Conan Doyle. In *The Doctrine of Repentance*, he is quoted as saying: "Till sin be bitter, Christ will not be sweet."[3]

The answer to the question, "How do I sin less?" is not, "Stop sinning," but rather, "Love God more." The well-known hymn by Augustus Toplady reads:

> *Rock of Ages, cleft for me,*
> *Let me hide myself in Thee;*
> *Let the water and the blood,*
> *From Thy wounded side which flowed,*
> *Be of sin the double cure;*
> *Save from wrath and make me pure.*[4]

The hymn writer, born more than one hundred years before Conan Doyle, said something profound when he wrote, "Be of sin the double cure."

God is the cure for our sinful heart.

The truth is that we cannot claim to love God and His Word and yet love what God hates and what His Word speaks against. We must aim to love God more than we love whatever sinful passion has fanned its flame in our heart.

Abstain from every form of evil.
1 THESSALONIANS 5:22 NASB

50.

HOLMES STUDY

"Education never ends, Watson. It is a series
of lessons with the greatest for the last."
THE ADVENTURE OF THE RED CIRCLE

The Baker Street Irregulars, the street children who acted as Holmes' undercover agents, proved to be a fixture in the canon. So it only makes sense that the most well-known society devoted to the study of Sherlock Holmes call themselves the *Baker Street Irregulars*.

According to their website, the literary society is dedicated to the study of Sherlock Holmes, Dr. Watson, Sir Arthur Conan Doyle, and the Victorian world.[1] They publish *The Baker Street Journal* and maintain The Baker Street Irregulars Trust. In short, the Baker Street Irregulars take their study of Sherlock Holmes seriously. How seriously? Make a joke about Sherlock Holmes only being a fictional character and watch the mayhem ensue. To a true Sherlockian, the great detective is more than a myth.

For more than one hundred years, fans of Sherlock Holmes have studied the great detective and never exhausted their analysis of him. New books are written all the time featuring the mastermind and his extraordinary powers of deduction. More than one hundred professional journals and newsletters are devoted to the great detective.

More has been written *about* Sherlock Holmes than Conan Doyle ever wrote *of* Sherlock Holmes.

And yet, the day will come when there is nothing new to discover about Sherlock Holmes, Dr. Watson, Conan Doyle, or the Victorian world. These subjects—fascinating as they may be—were never intended to be inexhaustible. At some point, should another hundred years pass, the newest members of the Baker Street Irregulars will either be writing entirely new stories featuring the detective or simply rehashing what has been discussed *ad nauseam.*

Whether or not Sherlockians want to admit it, Sherlock Holmes is not living and active. Not so with the study of spiritual things.

Our education about the mysteries of God will not end until we meet our Maker. And even in eternity, we will never know as much as God knows. "Oh, the depth of the riches and wisdom and knowledge of God! How unsearchable are his judgments and how inscrutable his ways!" (Romans 11:33 ESV). If we were guaranteed a thousand years of life on earth and we spent all of them in careful study and meditation of God, we still wouldn't know the half of who He is. Because of this—and because we are commanded to do so—we should make our study of God and His Word our greatest learning endeavor.

We should read the Bible, not to check it off on our to-do list, but to know God better. We should pray, not to bring our grocery list of wants and complaints to our heavenly Father, but to commune with God more deeply. We should study the commentaries of gifted theologians, not to sound smarter, but to become wiser.

We will never run out of things to learn about God. Because of this, we have no excuse not to learn something every day. Where we feel inadequate to the task of studying God's Word, we should ask Him to help us: "Open my eyes, that I may behold wondrous things out of your law" (Psalm 119:18 ESV).

It should be the aim of every child of God to know more about God today than we knew yesterday and more about God tomorrow than today. A wasted day is one in which we pillow our head having spent time studying everything without eternal consequence to the neglect of learning anything about our Savior.

The study of God is inexhaustible! We should aim to obey Colossians 3:2 and set our minds on things which are above.

What enables the Bible to be fresh and relevant to our lives thirty, fifty, or even one hundred years after we started reading it for the first time? Simply put: it is alive.

For the word of God is living and active, sharper than any two-edged sword, piercing to the division of soul

and of spirit, of joints and of marrow, and discerning
the thoughts and intentions of the heart.
HEBREWS 4:12 ESV

Excellent though Conan Doyle's writing is, he never promised it was a living book. Only the Bible has the right to make that claim. God's Word has the power to change lives because it is alive and active.

Every growing believer must be a student of the Bible.

Study to shew thyself approved unto God.
2 TIMOTHY 2:15 KJV

51.

THE IRON FIST

"I never make exceptions.
An exception disproves the rule."
THE SIGN OF FOUR

Arthur Conan Doyle's second novel, *The Sign of Four*, contains a complex plot involving the East India Company. It features stolen treasure and a secret pact between four convicts and two corrupt prison guards. The novel accomplishes a lot as it also gives us a closer look at Holmes' drug use and introduces us to Dr. Watson's future wife, Mary Morstan.

Perhaps the greatest gift to come from *The Sign of Four* is a conversation between Holmes and Watson early in the story. The two men are arguing about Mary Morstan, who has come to request the help of Sherlock Holmes. It is clear from the way Watson stands at the window and watches Morstan leave that this woman has already worked her way into the kind doctor's heart.

You can hear the lovesick tone in Watson's voice as he begins talking to Holmes about Morstan's beauty. Holmes, unsurprisingly, responds with his characteristic indifference, to which Watson says, "You really are an automaton—a calculating machine. There is something positively inhuman in you at times."[1] To which Holmes replies:

> *"The emotional qualities are antagonistic to clear reasoning. I assure you that the most winning woman I ever knew was hanged for poisoning three little children for their insurance-money, and the most repellent man of my acquaintance is a philanthropist who has spent nearly a quarter of a million upon the London poor."[2]*

Watson, still spellbound by Miss Morstan's beauty, says, "In this case however."[3] And Holmes utters the famous line: "I never make exceptions. An exception disproves the rule."[4] This quote from Sherlock Holmes is often repeated and characterizes him well.

The great detective's conviction that exceptions disprove the rule guided him as he made decisions and drew conclusions about his clients. Had he been more flexible with the people who visited him at 221B Baker Street, it is entirely possible we would not recognize the name *Sherlock Holmes* for its obscurity. How many detectives have tried and failed at their profession because they were willing to make allowances for nice or beautiful people?

So it goes for Christians. As believers, we should share this conviction about the inflexible truths of God.

Our society prizes tolerance above everything else. We are

taught that love and respect are the equivalent of acceptance. At first glance, this makes sense. Why should I have the right to draw negative conclusions about anyone else's choices? Who am I to say that anyone's opinions are wrong? And since God was gracious enough to include me in a family to which I did not naturally belong, I should be inclusive of everyone and everything, right?

Right. And wrong.

God Himself is the greatest example of tolerance. He has the right to wipe out the universe for our sinfulness, yet He is patient toward us, not willing that any should perish, but that all should come to repentance (see 2 Peter 3:9). The fruits of the Spirit include love, peace, patience, kindness, and gentleness, among others. Ephesians 4 commands us to bear with each other in love and with all patience and humility.

But this God-inspired tolerance draws a line.

Unfortunately, we live in a generation that has built a sacred shrine around personal opinion, so that whatever you think is right simply because you think it. This type of tolerance demands we accept every opinion as valid. To say that any opinion is wrong becomes *intolerance*.

A close look at scripture reveals the truth that God is intolerant about certain things and we should be, too.

"He who believes in the Son has eternal life;
but he who does not obey the Son will not see life,

but the wrath of God abides on him"
JOHN 3:36 NASB

Jesus said to him, "I am the way, and the truth, and the life. No one comes to the Father except through me."
JOHN 14:6 ESV

God is intolerant of sin and faithlessness.

God does not change His mind the way we do. We should be supremely grateful for this as it means we can bank on the changeless truths of God. God does not adjust with time and neither does His Gospel. The Word of God remains as true today as it was when it was written.

God's changelessness is one of the important aspects of His character that separates Him from man. As human beings, we change all the time.

It is intolerant to believe that Jesus Christ is the only way to God. The way people feel about that fact is far less significant than what they do in response to it.

Jesus Christ is the same yesterday, today, and forever.
HEBREWS 13:8 NLT

52.

FED UP

"It is of the highest importance to be able to recognize which facts are incidental and which are vital. Otherwise your energy and attention must be dissipated instead of concentrated."

THE ADVENTURE OF THE REIGATE SQUIRE

Sherlock Holmes was brilliant, but he wasn't always wise. One notable example of Holmes' foolishness is his addiction to cocaine and morphine. In *The Sign of Four* it becomes particularly evident that Holmes has a problem with drugs. Watson admits that he observed Holmes doing drugs three times a day over the course of many months. In no context is doing drugs three times a day over the course of many months a wise decision.

In Victorian London, morphine and cocaine were not illegal, but neither was their use viewed as a good idea. Watson pleaded with his friend to stop using the drugs, citing incalculable damage to the brain and the body. Holmes' explicit use of drugs proves intelligence and wisdom are vastly different things.

Another example of Holmes' imprudence is his decision to starve himself when he is working on a case. He believes not eating food will improve his ability to think. In "The Adventure of the Norwood Builder," Dr. Watson writes:

> *[Holmes] had no breakfast for himself, for it was one of his peculiarities that in his more intense moments he would permit himself no food, and I have known him to presume upon his iron strength until he has fainted from pure inanition.[1]*

No doubt there are better ways to pursue clear thinking.

Throughout the canon, Sherlock Holmes offers an untold number of lessons to his readers, many of which are pleasant and good. In the case of his drug use and starvation tactics, the lesson should be, "Don't do what I did."

As it pertains to wisdom versus knowledge, getting God's wisdom is infinitely more important than being smart. It has been said one hundred different ways: smart people know; wise people do. Scripture tells us that wisdom is the product of a single-minded pursuit of a relationship with God.

> *Blessed is the one who listens to me, watching daily at my gates, waiting beside my doors. For whoever finds me finds life and obtains favor from the LORD, but he who fails to find me injures himself; all who hate me love death.*
> PROVERBS 8:34–36 ESV

The good news is anyone—with any range of IQ—can pursue God's wisdom.

So what is wisdom, exactly? Proverbs 9:10 tells us that "the fear of the Lord is the beginning of wisdom, and the knowledge of the Holy One is insight" (ESV). Then, wisdom that is practical for life begins with knowing and fearing God. It changes the way we view all of the circumstances in our life. "Be not wise in your own eyes; fear the Lord, and turn away from evil. It will be healing to your flesh and refreshment to your bones" (Proverbs 3:7–8 ESV).

How do we know and fear God? We study the scriptures and we pray. God never commands us to do something without giving us the tools to accomplish it. In the case of pursuing wisdom, the tools God gives us for healthy relationship with Him are Bible reading, prayer, and godly counsel. Communion with God through prayer and study is the heartbeat of the Christian life. And throughout the scriptures, we are admonished to seek good counsel from people who love God.

No one should claim to be wise who does not spend regular time alone with God.

Oswald Chambers, a Scottish preacher who lived at the same time as Arthur Conan Doyle, wrote in his famous devotional, *My Utmost for His Highest*:

We tend to use prayer as a last resort, but God wants it to be our first line of defense. We pray when there's

nothing else we can do, but God wants us to pray before
we do anything at all.[2]

Perhaps, then, the greatest mark of a wise man is the ability to recognize his own foolishness and acknowledge God as the only solution to his problems. As we learn to know and fear God better, our prayer becomes *What I don't know, please teach me. What I don't have, please give me. What I am not, please make me.*

"But the wisdom from above is first pure, then peaceable, gentle, open to reason, full of mercy and good fruits, impartial and sincere" (James 3:17 ESV). If God's wisdom is pure, peacemaking, gentle, reasonable, merciful, fruitful, impartial, and genuine, then I have no right to be anything less.

The good news: in the face of our foolishness, God generously gives wisdom when we ask for it. In the history of humanity, no one has ever asked God for wisdom and been denied. God has given us everything we could possibly need to pursue His wisdom in this life.

If our primary goal in this life is to be smart, we will be anything but wise. We must determine to look at the circumstances in our life from God's perspective and respond accordingly.

*If any of you lacks wisdom, let him
ask God, who gives generously to all
without reproach, and it will be given him.*

JAMES 1:5 ESV

53

STATING THE OBVIOUS

"Let us know a little more before we act."
THE ADVENTURE OF THE ABBEY GRANGE

Dr. Watson is a loveable, loyal, down-to-earth man who serves as the contrast to the brilliant, nervous, eccentric Sherlock Holmes. So it is both funny and cringe-worthy when Watson decides to imitate Holmes' ability to see and deduct in "The Red-Headed League." With great enthusiasm, Watson writes:

> *I took a good look at the man and endeavoured, after the fashion of my companion, to read the indications which might be presented by his dress or appearance.*
>
> *I did not gain very much, however, by my inspection. . . Altogether, look as I would, there was nothing remarkable about the man save his blazing red head, and the expression of extreme chagrin and discontent upon his features.*[1]

In other words, Watson looked at Jabez Wilson, the London pawnbroker who came to Sherlock Holmes for help, and could only determine that Wilson was an unhappy red-headed man. Most of us—if put in the same situation—would likely have come to the same conclusions.

After Watson makes his simple deductions, Sherlock Holmes looks at Jabez Wilson and says:

> *"Beyond the obvious facts that he has at some time done manual labour, that he takes snuff, that he is a Freemason, that he has been in China, and that he has done a considerable amount of writing lately, I can deduce nothing else."*[2]

Really? That's all?

We can only imagine the deflated look that must have crossed Watson's face. For all of his genuine effort, he could not compete with Sherlock Holmes. He was never meant to compete with the great detective. He was meant to be the sincere, plodding sidekick.

Though Sherlock Holmes is an imaginary character, his skills at deduction teach us a helpful truth about life. As it pertains to people and situations, we would do well to observe, to *look closer*, before making assumptions or drawing conclusions. So often we observe only what takes little effort to see and then we give up.

Someone is unkind, and we assume it is personal. Someone is quiet, and we assume he doesn't care. Someone is emotional, and we assume she is weak. The list of possibilities is endless.

So how do we learn to make correct deductions in life? We listen carefully, wait expectantly, and respond intentionally.

Because life moves at the speed of light, it is easy to get swept up in conversations or situations that leave us wondering how we arrived at faulty conclusions. How often have we missed major clues or made major assumptions in a moment of weakness that have carried years of consequence or regret? We simply cannot know the burdens people are carrying if we choose to make assumptions instead of ask questions.

The Bible is not silent on this subject.

> *If one gives an answer before he hears,*
> *it is his folly and shame.*
> PROVERBS 18:13 ESV

> *Even a fool who keeps silent is considered wise;*
> *when he closes his lips, he is deemed intelligent.*
> PROVERBS 17:28 ESV

> *A fool takes no pleasure in understanding,*
> *but only in expressing his opinion.*
>
> PROVERBS 18:2 ESV

We must take careful, active steps in order to arrive at the right conclusions.

We must listen carefully. We must learn to really hear what people are saying to us. When someone offers a complaint to us or about us, we should strive to listen and not simply formulate a response or an excuse. Sometimes God uses sinful people with bad attitudes and wrong motives to speak truth into our lives. Thankfully, God can use even the weakness of men to accomplish good purposes in us. "Therefore consider carefully how you listen" (Luke 8:18 NIV).

We must wait expectantly. Waiting is not our natural impulse. Waiting implies someone else could act or talk or overhear while we delay. Someone else may beat us to the finish line of whatever goal we have while we are praying or seeking counsel. But waiting delays our impulsive responses or foolish reactions. Waiting can save us apologies and damaged testimonies. "But they who wait for the LORD shall renew their strength; they shall mount up with wings like eagles; they shall run and not be weary; they shall walk and not faint" (Isaiah 40:31 ESV).

We respond intentionally. We must exhibit the fruit of the Spirit if we belong to God. We should not say everything we are thinking or even half of what we feel. We should show the grace to others that we want given to us. "Let no corrupting talk come out of your mouths, but only such as is good for building up, as fits the occasion, that it may give grace to those who hear" (Ephesians 4:29 ESV).

While Dr. Watson was spouting off his elementary observations of Jabez Wilson, Sherlock Holmes was carefully, expectantly, intentionally drawing his own more impressive conclusions. It is no surprise that Holmes was right.

We should attempt to apply this same strategy when dealing with others. Learning to arrive at the right conclusions in life—by listening carefully, waiting expectantly, and responding intentionally—is great practice for making the right decisions about the Lord. There is, perhaps, no shorter track to spiritual destruction than coming to the wrong conclusions about God.

> *Everyone should be quick to listen,*
> *slow to speak and slow to become angry.*
> JAMES 1:19 NIV

54.

DOWNWARD BOUND

*"I must take the view that when a man embarks
upon a crime, he is morally guilty of any
other crime which may spring from it."*
THE ADVENTURE OF THE PRIORY SCHOOL

Sherlock Holmes' early adventures involved solving crimes like petty theft. As the stories continued, the crimes turned more dangerous and the choices continued in a downward spiral. As the stories got darker, so, too, did Sherlock Holmes.

Arguably the strangest Sherlock Holmes story in the canon is "The Adventure of the Cardboard Box," where Miss Susan Cushing receives a package in the mail containing two severed human ears packed in salt. The story was initially yanked from *The Memoirs of Sherlock Holmes* because of its controversial subject matter.

Perhaps surprisingly, the problem with the story was not the grotesque issue of the ears in the box or even the strange scene involving mind reading. The primary reason the story was offensive was because of its handling of the matter of adultery. Though the story is lacking the salacious details that most certainly would be included in current novels, the issue still exists.

Sherlock Holmes enthusiasts today call the issue "relatively mild" and claim readers will be more shocked over the packed ears than they will be the extramarital affair.

This is the pattern of sin.

As Christians, we are masters of making our sin prettier, aren't we? We call our evil choices "bad habits" or "weaknesses." We wink at our decisions and joke about our shortcomings. We defend our shortfalls by saying we are moody, insecure, tired, or hungry. We refer to our anger as "a temper" and to our lying as "embellishment." The only sins that really grieve us are the ones that belong to other people.

When "The Adventure of the Cardboard Box" was published in 1892, readers were shocked and appalled by Arthur Conan Doyle's flagrant attitude toward immorality. Today the story is published in nearly every collection of Sherlock Holmes' stories, and we laugh at the antiquated viewpoint of marital infidelity.

"They were only flirting!" today's reader might protest.

For the believer, sin should always grieve us. As we better understand God's Word, we should become more sensitive— not less—to the sins that destroy. "But each person is tempted when he is lured and enticed by his own desire. Then desire when it has conceived gives birth to sin, and sin when it is fully grown brings forth death" (James 1:14–15 ESV).

In a sin-cursed world, the decision to live a pure life will encounter many threats. Sadly, some of these threats will come from fellow believers in the body of Christ—people who understand God's expectations and choose to ignore them. This is why we must be aggressive as it pertains to the smallest amount of sin in our life. We are our own best accomplice when it comes to sinful choices. We make excuses for ourselves and rationalize whatever poor behavior in which we want to engage. But in the end, the sin will destroy us if it is left unchallenged.

Anything that we want more than we want to please God is sin, and sin has the power to break fellowship with the Father. We should learn to view sin the way God does so we can be right with Him. Our prayer should always and only be: "Let the words of my mouth and the meditation of my heart be acceptable in your sight, O LORD, my rock and my redeemer" (Psalm 19:14 ESV).

All is not lost for those who know and love God. "But thank God! He gives us victory over sin and death through our Lord Jesus Christ" (1 Corinthians 15:57 NLT).

At the end of "The Adventure of the Cardboard Box" is an interesting question, posed by the great detective, which goes unanswered. The final paragraph of the story reads:

> *"What is the meaning of it, Watson?" said Holmes solemnly as he laid down the paper. "What object is served by this circle of misery and violence and fear? It must tend to some end, or else our universe is ruled by chance, which is unthinkable. But what end? There is*

the great standing perennial problem to which human
reason is as far from an answer as ever."[1]

What is the meaning of life? We exist to bring God glory. Sin is a traitorous exchange for the glory of God. Which means sin in our life—in any form and at any time—should grieve us.

Thankfully, even after we have sinned, we have an opportunity to repair the broken relationship with our heavenly Father. For the child of God, no sin is greater than God's forgiveness.

For whoever keeps the whole law and yet stumbles
at just one point is guilty of breaking all of it.
JAMES 2:10 NIV

55.

CHARACTER MATTERS

"Jealousy is a strange transformer of characters."
THE ADVENTURE OF THE NOBLE BACHELOR

Sherlock Holmes is far from perfect. Despite the fact that the great detective is well loved (and he is!), it cannot escape our notice that he is also eccentric, moody, vain, and jealous. He cannot entertain the idea that he could ever be wrong, and he goes so far as to justify his unethical behavior if he thinks it will help him solve a case. As frustrating as these weaknesses can be, Arthur Conan Doyle's decision to make Sherlock Holmes human makes the character believable. As human beings we most identify with people or characters that are flawed.

The canon is filled to the brim with imperfect characters. In "The Adventure of the Noble Bachelor," for instance, a bride named Hatty disappears on the day of her wedding. She participates in the ceremony and then vanishes during the reception. The only strange occurrence at the wedding was a tiny mishap where Hatty dropped her wedding bouquet. No big deal. A gentleman in the front pew picked it up and handed it back to her.

All is well.

Except this little incident made all the difference. The man who returned the bouquet was a man from Hatty's past. One gem that came from "The Adventure of the Noble Bachelor" is a line spoken by Sherlock Holmes: "Jealousy is a strange transformer of characters."[1]

His words were a more eloquent way of saying: jealousy is catastrophic. And it is. Jealousy possesses the power of destruction. The Bible provides a horrifying word picture: "A tranquil heart gives life to the flesh, but envy makes the bones rot" (Proverbs 14:30 ESV).

We understand that jealousy isn't commendable, of course, but we certainly don't discuss our jealousy as "rotting of the bones."

God does. God sees our sin for what it is and what it has the potential to do to us. And He is a loving Father for being honest about our condition in His Word so that we can do something about it.

> *But if you have bitter jealousy and selfish ambition*
> *in your hearts, do not boast and be false to the truth.*
> *This is not the wisdom that comes down from above,*
> *but is earthly, unspiritual, demonic.*
> JAMES 3:14–15 ESV

As an oncologist is doing the noble thing by pointing out the smallest traces of cancer in the body and giving severe instructions on what to do about it, so a loving God is doing the same with regard to jealousy in our heart.

At the root of jealousy is self-centeredness. We think we deserve something that we have not been given. Perhaps we want praise, attention, or respect. Maybe, ironically, we covet opportunities to serve in the church. But whom are we truly seeking to serve when we envy other people who are using their gifts? Since God cannot be pleased by double-mindedness, we are surely seeking to serve ourselves and our own sinful ambition when we envy brothers and sisters in Christ.

The tiny spark of *I can do that better!* or *Why wasn't I given that opportunity?* can quickly become a destructive, widespread blaze if left unmanaged. This jealousy can destroy relationships and cripple our spiritual growth in the blink of an eye. Like the oncologist, God says to us, "Get rid of it!"

Jealousy over good opportunities is nothing new. Keep in mind Cain killed his brother, Abel, over an offering to God. The choice destroyed two lives and was consequential for countless others. God cannot be pleased with our offerings of service if our hearts are not right with Him, no matter how good or impressive our demonstration may appear to others.

Jealousy has the same power to destroy today as it has for thousands of years. So what should be our response to jealousy in the body of Christ?

So let no one boast in men. For all things are yours,
whether Paul or Apollos or Cephas or the world or life or
death or the present or the future—all are yours,
and you are Christ's, and Christ is God's.
1 Corinthians 3:21–23 esv

We should keep as our focus the reality that we, as God's children, will be given everything we need. "His divine power has granted to us all things that pertain to life and godliness, through the knowledge of him who called us to his own glory and excellence" (2 Peter 1:3 esv). If we have not been given something we desperately want, we can correctly assume God does not think we need it for now. "And my God will supply every need of yours according to his riches in glory in Christ Jesus" (Philippians 4:19 esv).

We must deal with jealousy before it destroys us.

For where jealousy and selfish ambition exist,
there is disorder and every evil thing.
James 3:16 nasb

56.

CONFESSION

"It is a capital mistake to theorize in advance of the facts."
THE ADVENTURE OF THE SECOND STAIN

Sherlock Holmes and Dr. John Watson first met in St. Bartholomew's Hospital, called St. Bart's for short. The oldest standing hospital in England, it survived the Great Fire of London and the Blitz in World War II. We first see Sherlock Holmes in the chemical lab from Dr. Watson's perspective:

> *At the sound of our steps he glanced round and sprang to his feet with a cry of pleasure.*
>
> *"I've found it! I've found it," he shouted to my companion, running towards us with a test-tube in his hand. "I have found a re-agent which is precipitated by hemoglobin, and by nothing else."[1]*

Though the scene reads a little bit like Greek for someone uninterested in medicine, the reality is that Sherlock Holmes has just created a blood test capable of analyzing a stain to determine whether or not it is blood. Though this type of test seems simplistic in our culture where DNA testing and blood typing is standard at a crime scene, in Victorian times,

Holmes' blood test was revolutionary, proving Conan Doyle was ahead of his time when he created the great detective.

But back to St. Bart's. Holmes and Watson first meet in the lab, seen in *A Study in Scarlet*, and in a humorous exchange, the two men—in an effort to determine if they would be compatible roommates—begin listing their personal faults. Holmes admits to keeping chemicals handy for conducting experiments. Watson discloses the fact that he owns a bull pup (which, ironically, we never see or hear about again). Holmes says:

> *"Let me see—what are my other shortcomings. I get in the dumps at times, and don't open my mouth for days on end. You must not think I am sulky when I do that. Just let me alone, and I'll soon be right. What have you to confess now? It's just as well for two fellows to know the worst of one another before they begin to live together."*[2]

Eventually, Holmes confesses that he runs a consulting detective agency and that his apartment will be filled with guests at all hours who need his assistance. The admissions seem to be of no consequence to Dr. Watson. The pair decides to board together, and one of the most famous friendships in literary history is born.

Holmes was on to something when he suggested that he and Watson share their faults in order to determine their compatibility. Where most people would probably prefer to put a best foot forward in an interview, sharing strengths as opposed to weaknesses, this pair got to the heart of the matter and shared the issues that would prevent a healthy companionship.

Dietrich Bonhoeffer was a German pastor, theologian, and Nazi protester who wrote at the same time Conan Doyle was writing. He once explained:

> *He who is alone with his sin is utterly alone. It may be that Christians, notwithstanding corporate worship, common prayer, and all their fellowship in service, may still be left to their loneliness. The final break-through to fellowship does not occur, because, though they have fellowship with one another as believers and as devout people, they do not have fellowship as the undevout, as sinners. The pious fellowship permits no one to be a sinner. So everybody must conceal his sin from himself and from the fellowship. We dare not be sinners. Many Christians are unthinkably horrified when a real sinner is suddenly discovered among the righteous. So we remain alone with our sin, living in lies and hypocrisy. The fact is that we are sinners![3]*

What truth and freedom exist in Bonhoeffer's words!

While most Christians would be hard-pressed to deny

that they are sinners—given the massive evidence to the contrary in life and in the pages of scripture—so, too, most Christians today would find confession to another believer to be impossibly difficult. We worry what people will think of us, and we fear we could lose the shine on our carefully manicured image. Fear of man replaces fear of God, and we prefer to stay silent about the sin in our hearts even if it means we are unable to overcome it.

The truth is that sin works best in secret. When we are caught in a pattern of sin and we choose to separate ourselves from other believers as a result, the sin has incredible power to destroy us. It would appear to be the kindness of God, then, and not a desire to shame us, that He tosses a life jacket in the form of confession into the swirling waters of our sinful secrets.

When God gives us a command, we can safely assume it is for our good.

> *Confess your sins to each other and pray for each other so that you may be healed. The earnest prayer of a righteous person has great power and produces wonderful results.*
> JAMES 5:16 NLT

57.

A MYSTERIOUS SOCIETY

"My name is Sherlock Holmes. It is my business
to know what other people don't know."
THE ADVENTURE OF THE BLUE CARBUNCLE

Fans of Sherlock Holmes take the detective stories—all of them—seriously.

This is a wild understatement.

A casual search of the Internet will reveal hundreds of societies, fan clubs, and publications around the world dedicated to the love and study of Sherlock Holmes. Some groups are closed to women, other groups meet underground, and still others remain invite-only.

The premier Holmes society in the world, The Baker Street Irregulars—named for the ragtag team of children who assisted Holmes—gifts an "irregular shilling" membership into the society to people who have done something extraordinary in a Sherlockian publication.[1] This group has published *The Baker Street Journal* since 1946. Two notable honorary members and Sherlock enthusiasts included Franklin D. Roosevelt and Harry S. Truman.

A true Sherlockian is someone who studies and appreciates the writing of Sir Arthur Conan Doyle and learns everything possible about Sherlock Holmes. Furthermore, the secret to discovering a Holmes enthusiast is to say something about Sherlock Holmes and watch for responses. A Sherlockian's eyes will inevitably light up at the mention of the great detective, and the tiniest detail will carry tremendous significance.

Don't believe it? Just mention Sherlock Holmes' famous deerstalker cap or calabash pipe and watch what happens. The Sherlockian in the room will be the first to speak up and tell you that neither appeared in the actual writing of Arthur Conan Doyle.

To a Sherlockian, every bit of the canon matters. Christians should not be outdone in their love of the Bible by fans of fiction.

What we hold in our hands via the scriptures will last forever. Conan Doyle's canon is an impressive work of fiction, but it makes no promises to live forever. Sad, isn't it, that followers of Christ could be outdone in their enthusiasm by followers of Holmes? And yet it happens all the time. While fans of Holmes are eagerly reading stories, comparing notes, studying details, and sparking conversations, Bibles are gathering dust in Christian homes all over the world, and believers are afraid to start the conversation about God. Enthusiasm for the Bible has been replaced by inactivity, and fear of offense has replaced zeal.

First Peter 3:15 exhorts believers to know and defend what they believe to be true about Jesus Christ:

But in your hearts honor Christ the Lord as holy, always being prepared to make a defense to anyone who asks you for a reason for the hope that is in you; yet do it with gentleness and respect (ESV).

We are often admonished to be prepared to make a defense. Pastors and Bible teachers spend ample time instructing us to this end. Prior to that appeal, though, is a simple phrase that is often overlooked in the rush to get to the end of the verse: "But in your hearts honor Christ the Lord as holy."

Perhaps one reason we fail to give a proper defense when asked is because the foundation of our apologetics—honoring Christ in our own heart—is weak. How can we possibly give a reason for the hope that is in us if no one recognizes we have a hope within us? Worse yet, what if we don't genuinely hope in God?

Honoring Christ the Lord as holy indicates respect, obedience, and worship. He has every authority to demand our heart, and we have every obligation to submit it to Him.

If honoring Christ as Lord is purely an intellectual exercise, it will show in the way we talk—or don't talk—about our faith. Many believers complain that it is hard to articulate their convictions to other people. And in a culture that often bullies the Christian faith, it is easy to understand how a child of God might feel tongue-tied when asked a question or invited to explain a belief. But when hope drives the conversation because Christ is honored as Lord, no longer is the discussion a matter of sticking to a script or worrying about what the other person thinks. Now it's an opportunity to discuss what Jesus did for us.

Blessed be the God and Father of our Lord Jesus Christ!
According to his great mercy, he has caused us to
be born again to a living hope through the resurrection
of Jesus Christ from the dead.
1 PETER 1:3 ESV

Knowing facts about someone versus loving someone is as different as reading names in a phone book versus discussing a favored family member. It will show in the way that we talk, and more importantly, in the way that we live.

We cannot be God-centered if we refuse to be Word-centered. God has given us the scriptures as a means to know and love Him more. If we are not spending time reading God's Word, how can we possibly pretend to be right with Him?

But whose delight is in the law of the LORD,
and who meditates on his law day and night.
PSALM 1:2 NIV

58.

THE DEADLY SIN

"For once you have fallen so low.
Let us see in the future how high you can rise."
THE ADVENTURE OF THE THREE STUDENTS

Perhaps one of the greatest ironies about Sherlock Holmes is how dedicated he was to achieving justice while at the same time being willing to cross ethical lines to get his goals accomplished. Holmes demonstrated time and again that he believed the end justifies the means. Holmes knew he was good at what he did, and he was willing to stop at nothing to win.

One of his favorite pastimes was to baffle the inspectors with his superior skills at deduction and crime solving. In thirty-two stories in the canon, Holmes is called upon to work with the London police on a case. To Holmes' mind, it would seem he considered it a competition to see who could solve the case. Surprisingly, he often allowed the officer to take the credit for identifying the criminal in the end.

Being right is vastly more important to Sherlock Holmes than what anyone thinks of him. Because of his impressive abilities, Holmes' most noteworthy clients included a prime minister and a king—both of whom consulted Holmes because he was the best in his field. Holmes was unwilling—or perhaps even incapable—of working agreeably with the local police to solve crimes. He spoke his mind and played by his own rules. Though they had the same goals—identifying wrongdoers—they had different methods and motivations and arrived at their conclusions in infinitely different ways. Had he been asked, Holmes might have explained that crime solving was more important to him than harmony with law enforcement.

Though Holmes' peacemaking skills leave much to be desired, we could learn a thing or two from his adherence to truth. As it pertains to getting the facts right, Holmes has a razor-sharp focus and a one-track mind.

The Bible is clear that Christians should be kind to one other, but it is also clear that unity that denies doctrinal purity is not God's expectation for our lives. Purity of doctrine should never be sacrificed as a means of maintaining Christian unity. Our thoughts may include:

But if I speak up, I could lose friends.

If I am the only one in the room with that opinion, I might feel awkward.

What if people think I am trying to act like a spiritual authority?

The Bible answers these concerns with this plea:

*I appeal to you, brothers, to watch out for those who
cause divisions and create obstacles contrary to the
doctrine that you have been taught; avoid them.
For such persons do not serve our Lord Christ,
but their own appetites, and by smooth talk and
flattery they deceive the hearts of the naive.*
ROMANS 16:17–18 ESV

The people in our lives who cross doctrinal lines and create divisions are either genuinely mistaken and will be willing to receive wise counsel, or else they are intentionally deceiving hearts and need to be avoided.

The Bible leaves no room for apathy concerning doctrinal error. One of the qualifications for a leader in the church is: "He must hold firm to the trustworthy word as taught, so that he may be able to give instruction in sound doctrine and also to rebuke those who contradict it" (Titus 1:9 ESV). Teaching good doctrine and censuring bad doctrine are requirements to lead.

Many Christians choose to take sides, joining either the "biblical accuracy" or the "relational harmony" team, but as Christians we should endeavor to do both. We should love truth and love people, understanding that in some ways, these goals are one and the same. "Little children, let us not love in word or talk but in deed and in truth" (1 John 3:18 ESV).

When a situation or confrontation forces us to make the choice between harmony and accuracy, we must fulfill our biblical obligation to lovingly choose biblical accuracy. Sacrificing God's truth to maintain peace is not God's desire.

Standing for truth in this age is not always an easy task. Our Western culture often views truth telling as intolerance or bigotry. Because of this and in spite of this, doctrinal vigilance in the church and in the home is of critical importance. Thanks to media, education, books, and relationships, one thousand voices clamor for real estate in our thinking every day. Some of these voices speak truth. Others speak inaccuracies from a genuinely mistaken perspective. Still others want to lead us astray and use winsome words to accomplish their dark purposes. The aim of the believer is to cling to doctrinal truth and carefully discern who fits in which categories and respond accordingly.

To the one thousand voices that speak into our lives every day, we ought to respond out of love and desire for the truth and not out of pride or anger.

Follow the pattern of the sound words that you have heard from me, in the faith and love that are in Christ Jesus. By the Holy Spirit who dwells within us, guard the good deposit entrusted to you.
2 TIMOTHY 1:13–14 ESV

59

PERSON OF INTEREST

*"Professor Moriarty is not a man who
lets the grass grow under his feet."*
THE FINAL PROBLEM

Professor Moriarty was created for one purpose: to destroy Sherlock Holmes. If Sherlock Holmes is the great mastermind detective, Professor Moriarty is the great fictional master criminal. Some canon enthusiasts believe Moriarty represents what Holmes would be if he had turned to the dark side instead of fighting for justice.

According to legend, Moriarty was based on a real man, Adam Worth, who lived in the late 1800s. He was a brilliant, ambitious criminal who became the most successful safecracker and bank robber in New York City. Conan Doyle couldn't have picked a better prototype for Professor Moriarty. Adam Worth was called *the Napoleon of Crime*.

In "The Final Problem," Holmes is talking to Watson about Professor Moriarty when he says of the great master criminal:

*"He is a man of good birth and excellent education,
endowed by nature with a phenomenal mathematical*

faculty. . . But the man had hereditary tendencies of the most diabolical kind. A criminal strain ran in his blood, which, instead of being modified, was increased and rendered infinitely more dangerous by his extraordinary mental powers. . . He is the Napoleon of crime, Watson. He is the organizer of half that is evil and of nearly all that is undetected in this great city."[1]

The Napoleon of crime. Sound like Moriarty? Many readers believe so.

When Conan Doyle decided to leave Sherlock Holmes and move on to his other literary pursuits, he created Professor Moriarty to kill the great detective. If Moriarty could destroy Sherlock Holmes, the massive fan base would stop asking for more adventures of Sherlock Holmes, and Doyle could finally write something else.

But just as Sherlock Holmes was bigger than life, so, too, Professor Moriarty took on a life and personality of his own and became the famous archenemy of the great detective. In many ways, Moriarty is responsible for making Holmes a hero.

When Conan Doyle brought Holmes back to life, he brought the influence of Moriarty back with him. Moriarty is only seen in two of Conan Doyle's stories—"The Final Problem" and *The Valley of Fear*, and yet in many ways, he plays a role in all of the stories. Readers know to be suspicious of the master criminal, watching for where he might turn up next. Whenever something evil occurs in one of the stories, the astute reader can't help but ask, *Was Moriarty involved?* Or perhaps more accurately, *How was Moriarty involved?*

Thankfully, Professor James Moriarty is a fictional character whose influence is limited to the printed page, but the evil professor taught us one thing: where there is good, there is evil.

Christians must be suspicious of the Great Deceiver. As believers, we cannot minimize the danger of our great enemy. Satan wants nothing more than to see the testimony of Christ destroyed in our lives and ministry. And just as Professor Moriarty did not play by the rules, so, too, our enemy stops at nothing to see his plans accomplished.

Put on the full armor of God, so that you will be able to stand firm against the schemes of the devil.
Ephesians 6:11 NASB

Stay alert! Watch out for your great enemy, the devil. He prowls around like a roaring lion, looking for someone to devour.
1 Peter 5:8 NLT

When Satan is called *the lion*, we should sense his strength and brutality. His capabilities shouldn't be laughed off or reduced to Halloween decorations or cartoon sketches. And though he cannot destroy us if we belong to God, Satan can do enough damage with his tools of fear and intimidation to stunt us in our growth and prevent us from useful service on earth.

The unfortunate reality about coming face-to-face with a lion who wants to destroy us is that we will be destroyed unless we have something on our side that is bigger and more powerful than the lion. The good news is that God is bigger than our Professor Moriarty, and the last chapter for the devil has already been written. Martin Luther summed it up well when he penned the words to his famous hymn, "A Mighty Fortress Is Our God":

> *And though this world, with devils filled, should*
> *threaten to undo us,*
> > *We will not fear, for God hath willed his truth to*
> > *triumph through us.*
> > > *The Prince of Darkness grim, we tremble not for him;*
> > > *His rage we can endure, for lo, his doom is sure;*
> > > *One little word shall fell him.[2]*

> *The thief comes only to steal and kill and destroy.*
> *I came that they may have life and have it abundantly.*
> JOHN 10:10 ESV

60.

IN THE END

"Data! Data! Data! I can make no bricks without clay."
THE ADVENTURE OF THE COPPER BEECHES

Damsels in distress are not uncommon in the adventures of Sherlock Holmes. Many of Conan Doyle's stories feature women who are at their wit's end with fear or anguish—and enough of Holmes' clientele are women that it raises suspicions as to whether or not the detective dislikes women as much as he wants people to think he does. Perhaps the detective doth protest too much.

In "The Adventure of the Copper Beeches," it would appear that Holmes was beginning to like Miss Violet Hunter as more than a client. Miss Hunter is described as "plainly but neatly dressed, with a bright, quick face, freckled like a plover's egg, and with the brisk manner of a woman who has had her own way to make in the world."[1] For a brief instant, it looks promising. Then at the end of the story, Dr. Watson says simply: "As to Miss Violet Hunter, my friend Holmes, rather to my disappointment, manifested no further interest in her when once she had ceased to be the centre of one of his problems."[2]

As seemed to be the natural pattern for our beloved detective,

Holmes dismissed Hunter as just another pretty problem and moved on to the next case.

Holmes' interaction with Miss Violet Hunter was not entirely in vain. One of the best-known quotes from the canon came from this case. Holmes, trying to think through the strange details of the situation involving Miss Hunter, is sitting alone "with knitted brows and an abstracted air" when he cries, "Data! Data! Data! I can make no bricks without clay."[3]

This statement almost certainly refers to the Old Testament account of the children of Israel who were enslaved by Pharaoh and commanded to make bricks without straw. One of the most frustrating scenarios for the people of God is recorded in Exodus:

> *So the taskmasters and the foremen of the people went out and said to the people, "Thus says Pharaoh, 'I will not give you straw. Go and get your straw yourselves wherever you can find it, but your work will not be reduced in the least.'"*
> *So the people were scattered throughout all the land of Egypt to gather stubble for straw.*
> Exodus 5:10–12 esv

Exodus 5 and 6 record a difficult time in the Israelites' history when they suffered in Egypt under harsh slavery. The command to make bricks without straw was not the result of Egypt not having straw, but of Pharaoh not having mercy.

Understandably, the Israelites had a broken spirit.

As children of God, we experience a broken spirit when we think we are being forced to do the impossible. Maintaining the proper testimony under pressure or standing up for what we believe in the face of potential job loss can be terrifying. How can we be expected to trust God for our needs while the bills pile up or the cancer spreads?

We read about people like Meriam Yahia Ibrahim, the Sudanese woman sentenced to die for refusing to deny Christ, and we think, *That is expecting bricks without clay. How could God ask her to do that?*

The answer: As believers, we have not been called to live the Christian life without the proper tools to make it happen. God, in His unfathomable kindness, has given us everything we need to live lives that bring Him honor in every situation. As He strengthened Ibrahim in jail and as He provided for the children of Israel, so He empowers us to accomplish whatever tasks are put in front of us. "Fear not, for I am with you; be not dismayed, for I am your God; I will strengthen you, I will help you, I will uphold you with my righteous right hand" (Isaiah 41:10 ESV).

Not only do we have prayer and Bible reading at our disposal, but we have the potential for godly friendships and healthy churches. The icing on the cake is centuries of psalms, hymns, and spiritual songs that have been passed down through generations.

We, as the people of God, have not been left to make bricks without clay.

Knowing the conclusion to the story of Pharaoh and the Israelites, it is difficult to read Exodus and not cry, "Remember how this ends!" The same might be true for future generations who read of Meriam Yahia Ibrahim, who was released after extensive negotiations. "Remember how this ends!"

In a much less significant way, it can be said for readers of the canon who have just finished "The Final Problem" for the first time and believe their much-loved detective has fallen to his death over Reichenbach Falls. "Remember how this ends!"

The same can be said for us in whatever situation we are currently facing: *Remember how this ends!*

"The Adventure of the Retired Colourman" is the last of Conan Doyle's stories about Sherlock Holmes. It seems fitting that this last chapter was written about Holmes and Watson in December, at the close of a year. Both Holmes and Watson are in their seventies, reflecting on a good career and solid partnership, when they discover a new case—an opportunity to solve the mystery of a cold-blooded killer.

In true Conan Doyle style, a final mystery involving Carina remains, to this day, unsolved.

It is particularly fitting because Sherlock Holmes continues to live in the hearts and minds of readers around the globe. And in the same way that Doyle did not actually close the book on Holmes and Watson, neither have those who love them best. The final words of the final story read: "You can file it in our archives, Watson. Some day the true story may be told."[4]

For each of us, the day is coming when our true story will be told. Let's live so as to give someone something worthy to read.

His divine power has granted to us all things that pertain to life and godliness, through the knowledge of him who called us to his own glory and excellence.
2 PETER 1:3 ESV

COMPLETE LIST OF
SHERLOCK HOLMES STORIES
BY ARTHUR CONAN DOYLE

NOVELS

1. *A Study in Scarlet*
2. *The Sign of the Four*
3. *The Hound of the Baskervilles*
4. *The Valley of Fear*

SHORT STORIES

The Adventures of Sherlock Holmes
1. "A Scandal in Bohemia"
2. "The Adventure of the Red-Headed League"
3. "A Case of Identity"
4. "The Boscombe Valley Mystery"
5. "The Five Orange Pips"
6. "The Man with the Twisted Lip"
7. "The Adventure of the Blue Carbuncle"
8. "The Adventure of the Speckled Band"
9. "The Adventure of the Engineer's Thumb"
10. "The Adventure of the Noble Bachelor"
11. "The Adventure of the Beryl Coronet"
12. "The Adventure of the Copper Beeches"

The Memoirs of Sherlock Holmes

1. "Silver Blaze"
2. "The Adventure of the Cardboard Box"
3. "The Adventure of the Yellow Face"
4. "The Adventure of the Stockbroker's Clerk"
5. "The Adventure of the Gloria Scott"
6. "The Adventure of the Musgrave Ritual"
7. "The Adventure of the Reigate Squire"
8. "The Adventure of the Crooked Man"
9. "The Adventure of the Resident Patient"
10. "The Adventure of the Greek Interpreter"
11. "The Adventure of the Naval Treaty"
12. "The Final Problem"

The Return of Sherlock Holmes

1. "The Adventure of the Empty House" (the return of Holmes)
2. "The Adventure of the Norwood Builder"
3. "The Adventure of the Dancing Men"
4. "The Adventure of the Solitary Cyclist"
5. "The Adventure of the Priory School"
6. "The Adventure of Black Peter"
7. "The Adventure of Charles Augustus Milverton"
8. "The Adventure of the Six Napoleons"
9. "The Adventure of the Three Students"
10. "The Adventure of the Golden Pince-Nez"

SOURCES

1. THE ART OF LISTENING
    1. Sir Arthur Conan Doyle, *The Complete Sherlock Holmes* (New York: Barnes and Noble, 2009), 849.

    2. Ibid., 857.

2. DEATH OF A DETECTIVE
    1. Sir Arthur Conan Doyle, *The Complete Sherlock Holmes* (New York: Barnes and Noble, 2009), 5.

    2. Ibid.

    3. Ibid., 20.

    4. C. S. Lewis, *Reflections on the Psalms* (New York: Mariner Books, 1964), 94–95.

3. MAN BEHIND THE MASK
    1. Sir Arthur Conan Doyle, *The Complete Sherlock Holmes* (New York: Barnes and Noble, 2009), 151.

    2. Ibid., 159.

    3. Ibid., 146.

4. AN UNLIKELY FRIENDSHIP
    1. Sir Arthur Conan Doyle, *The Complete Sherlock Holmes* (New York: Barnes and Noble, 2009), 611.

    2. Stephen Edmondson, *Calvin's Christology* (Cambridge: Cambridge University Press, 2004), 92.

5. Meeting Mycroft

1. Sir Arthur Conan Doyle, *The Complete Sherlock Holmes* (New York: Barnes and Noble, 2009), 406.

2. Ibid., 407.

3. http://www.mysterynet.com holmes/22greekinterpreter/

4. https://books.google.com/books?id=zRqIKEKectUC&pg-=PA200&dq=to+verify+his+own+solutions&hl-=en&sa=X&ei+odQlVdy-EIXZsAWRx4CACg&ved-=0CEoQ6AEwCA#v= onepage&q=to%20 verify%20his%20own%20solutions&f=false

6. Hooked

1. Sir Arthur Conan Doyle, *The Complete Sherlock Holmes* (New York: Barnes and Noble, 2009), 981.

2. Ibid., 991.

3. https://ebooks.adelaide.edu.au/d/doyle/arthur_ conan/d75ca/chapter4.html

7. Game of Proof

1. Sir Arthur Conan Doyle, *The Complete Sherlock Holmes* (New York: Barnes and Noble, 2009), 96.

8. The Power of Restraint

1. Sir Arthur Conan Doyle, *The Complete Sherlock Holmes* (New York: Barnes and Noble, 2009), 323.

2. "And Now, a Word from Arthur Conan Doyle,"
    BSI Annual Dinner Talk 1989. Accessed November
    24, 2014. http://www.bsiarchivalhistory.org/BSI_
    Archival_History/ACD_Word.html.

9. Observation Skills

1. Sir Arthur Conan Doyle, *The Complete Sherlock
    Holmes* (New York: Barnes and Noble, 2009), 165.

2. Leslie S. Klinger and John le Carré, *The New Annotated
    Sherlock Holmes, Volume 1, The Adventures of Sherlock
    Holmes & the Memoirs of Sherlock Holmes* (New York:
    W.W. Norton & Company, Inc., 2007), 57.

3. Sir Arthur Conan Doyle, *The Complete Sherlock
    Holmes* (New York: Barnes and Noble, 2009), 168.

10. Home Sweet Holmes

1. Sir Arthur Conan Doyle, *The Complete Sherlock Holmes*
    (New York: Barnes and Noble, 2009), 458.

2. John Bunyan, *Justification by an Imputed Righteousness*.
    (n.d.; Acacia John Bunyan Online Library) Accessed
    November 24, 2014. http://truthinheart.com/Early
    OberlinCD/CD/Bunyan/text/Justification.Imputed.
    Right/Entire.Book.html.

11. A Study in Silence

1. Sir Arthur Conan Doyle, *The Complete Sherlock
    Holmes* (New York: Barnes and Noble, 2009), 213.

2. Ibid., 215.

14. AGE OF REASON
   1. Sir Arthur Conan Doyle, *The Complete Sherlock Holmes* (New York: Barnes and Noble, 2009), 338.

15. THE MAIL MAYHEM
   1. Sir Arthur Conan Doyle, *The Complete Sherlock Holmes* (New York: Barnes and Noble, 2009), 313.
   2. Ibid., 958.

16. THICKER THAN BLOOD
   1. Sir Arthur Conan Doyle, The Complete Sherlock Holmes (New York: Barnes and Noble, 2009), 449.
   2. Dan Hartland, "*The Best and Wisest Man Who I Have Ever Known,*" @ Number 71(blog), May 27, 2009, https://thestoryandthetruth.wordpress.com/tag/the-final-problem/.

17. MOTHER KNOWS BEST
   1. Jack Goldstein and Isabella Reese, *101 Amazing Facts about Arthur Conan Doyle* (Luton:/Andrew U.K. Limited, 2014), Fact 39.
   2. Sir Arthur Conan Doyle, *The Complete Sherlock Holmes* (New York: Barnes and Noble, 2009), 449.

18. PLAYING FAVORITES
   1. Sir Arthur Conan Doyle, *The Complete Sherlock Holmes* (New York: Barnes and Noble, 2009), 478.

2. http://www.brainyquote.com/quotes/quotes/m/
marktwain131229.html.

19. By Mistake

1. Sir Arthur Conan Doyle, *The Complete Sherlock Holmes* (New York: Barnes and Noble, 2009), 267.

20. Matron of Honor

1. Sir Arthur Conan Doyle, *The Complete Sherlock Holmes* (New York: Barnes and Noble, 2009), 892.

21. The Prince of Crime

1. Sir Arthur Conan Doyle, *The Complete Sherlock Holmes* (New York: Barnes and Noble, 2009), 12.

2. Ibid.

3. http://www.worlds-best-detective-crime-and-murder-mystery-books.com/poeinfluenceondoyle01-article.html

4. Sir Arthur Conan Doyle, *The Complete Sherlock Holmes* (New York: Barnes and Noble, 2009), 12.

5. Ibid.

22. Justice for Hire

1. Sir Arthur Conan Doyle, *The Complete Sherlock Holmes* (New York: Barnes and Noble, 2009), 544.

23. Fulcrum Files

1. Sir Arthur Conan Doyle, *The Complete Sherlock Holmes* (New York: Barnes and Noble, 2009), 939.

2. Ibid., 7.

3. "Yesterday, Today, Forever," accessed November 26, 2014, http://library.timelesstruths.org/music/Yesterday_Today_Forever/.

4. "The Solid Rock," accessed November 26, 2014, http://library.timelesstruths.org/music/The_Solid_Rock/.

24. ON PURPOSE

1. Sir Arthur Conan Doyle, *The Complete Sherlock Holmes* (New York: Barnes and Noble, 2009), 173.

2. "Only One Life, Twill Soon Be Past - Poem by C.T. Studd," *Poetry About Jesus and Salvation*, accessed February 11, 2015, http://cavaliersonly.com/poetry_by_christian_poets_of_the_past/only_one_life_twill_soon_be_past_-_poem_by_ct_studd.

26. GOOD CHEMISTRY

1. Sir Arthur Conan Doyle, *The Complete Sherlock Holmes* (New York: Barnes and Noble, 2009), 23.

27. CRIME 101

1. Sir Arthur Conan Doyle, *The Complete Sherlock Holmes* (New York: Barnes and Noble, 2009), 27.

28. CLASS ACT

   1. Sir Arthur Conan Doyle, *The Complete Sherlock Holmes* (New York: Barnes and Noble, 2009), 111.

   2. Ibid., 29.

   3. Ibid., 301.

29. TRUTH AND CONSEQUENCES

   1. "Sherlock Holmes Awarded Title for Most Portrayed Literary Human Character in Film & TV," Guinness World Records, May 14, 2012, accessed November 23, 2014, http://www.guinnessworldrecords.com/news/2012/5/sherlock-holmes-awarded-title-for-most-portrayed-literary-human-character-in-film-tv-41743/.

   2. Vincent Starrett, *The Private Life of Sherlock Holmes* (New York:/Otto Penzler Books, 1993), 156.

   3. Sir Arthur Conan Doyle, *The Complete Sherlock Holmes* (New York: Barnes and Noble, 2009), 328.

   4. Ibid., 336.

30. THE MORIARTY EFFECT

   1. Sir Arthur Conan Doyle, *The Complete Sherlock Holmes* (New York: Barnes and Noble, 2009), 440.

   2. Ibid.

31. THE MASTER PLAN

1. Sir Arthur Conan Doyle, *The Complete Sherlock Holmes* (New York: Barnes and Noble, 2009), 199.

2. "Charles Darwin Views on God, Religion, and Religious Belief from His Autobiography and Letters," accessed November 25, 2014, http://www.age-of-the-sage.org/philosophy/darwin_god_religion_religious_belief.html.

32. THE MIND'S EYE

1. Sir Arthur Conan Doyle, *The Complete Sherlock Holmes* (New York: Barnes and Noble, 2009), 425–426.

2. Ibid.

3. Ibid., 11.

33. THE GRAND FINALE

1. Steven Doyle and David A. Crowder, *Sherlock Holmes for Dummies* (Hoboken, New Jersey: Wiley Publishing, 2010), 55.

2. Sir Arthur Conan Doyle, *The Complete Sherlock Holmes* (New York: Barnes and Noble, 2009), 435.

34. SURVIVAL GUIDE

1. Sir Arthur Conan Doyle, *The Complete Sherlock Holmes* (New York: Barnes and Noble, 2009), 661.

2. "The Big Read," *BBC*, April 2003, accessed November 26, 2014, http://www.bbc.co.uk/arts/bigread/top200.shtml.

3. Charles Spurgeon, "Justification by Grace." accessed November 26, 2014, http://www.spurgeon.org/sermons/0126.htm.

35. Balancing Act
    1. Sir Arthur Conan Doyle, *The Complete Sherlock Holmes* (New York: Barnes and Noble, 2009), 8.

36. For the Love
    1. Sir Arthur Conan Doyle, *The Complete Sherlock Holmes* (New York: Barnes and Noble, 2009), 145.

    2. Ibid., 152.

37. Death Grip
    1. Sir Arthur Conan Doyle, *The Complete Sherlock Holmes* (New York: Barnes and Noble, 2009), 245.

    2. Ibid., 8.

    3. Ibid., 245.

    4. Ibid., 327.

38. Next to Godliness
    1. "Habits and Personality," accessed November 26, 2014, http://sherlockholmes101.weebly.com/habits-and-personality.html.

    2. Sir Arthur Conan Doyle, *The Complete Sherlock Holmes* (New York: Barnes and Noble, 2009), 704.

    3. Sir Arthur Conan Doyle, *The Complete Sherlock Holmes* (New York: Barnes and Noble, 2009), 361.

    4. John Wesley, *A Collection of Hymns, for the Use of the People called Methodists* (London, 1779).

39. FORGET IT
    1. Sir Arthur Conan Doyle, *The Complete Sherlock Holmes* (New York: Barnes and Noble, 2009), 9.

    2. Ibid.

41. THE NOT-SO-HUMBLE HOLMES
    1. Sir Arthur Conan Doyle, *The Complete Sherlock Holmes* (New York: Barnes and Noble, 2009), 401.

    2. Dallas Willard, *The Spirit of the Disciplines: Understanding How God Changes Lives* (New York: HarperCollins, 1988), 173.

    3. Andrew Murray, *The Wisdom of Andrew Murray, Vol. 1* (Virginia: Wilder Publications), 40.

42. THE SINCEREST FORM OF FLATTERY
    1. *Unlocking Sherlock* (BBC, 2014), accessed November 26, 2014, http://www.netflix.com/WiMovie/70306403?trkid=13752289.

    2. http://www.sherlockholmesonline.org/SherlockHolmes/. Accessed 26 November 2014.

    3. Sir Arthur Conan Doyle, *The Complete Sherlock Holmes* (New York: Barnes and Noble, 2009), 307.

    4. Charles Hodge, *Commentary on Second Corinthians*

(Grand Rapids: Wm. B. Eerdmans Publishing, 1994), 133.

43. A MATTER OF PERSPECTIVE

1. Sir Arthur Conan Doyle, *The Complete Sherlock Holmes* (New York: Barnes and Noble, 2009), 8.

44. CRIME FILES

1. T. S. Eliot, in a review of *The Complete Sherlock Holmes Short Stories*, 1929. Accessed November 26, 2014, http://thenorwoodbuilder.tumblr.com/post/39500244240/dan-andriacco-t-s-eliot-and-sherlock-holmes.

2. C. S. Lewis, *Mere Christianity* (Grand Rapids: Zondervan, 1952), 136–137.

3. Jonathan Edwards, *The Works of President Edwards in Four Volumes: A Reprint of the Worcester Edition, with Valuable Additions and a Copious General Index, Vol. 4* (New York:/Leavitt, Trow, & Company, 1844), 578.

45. MIND OVER MATTER

1. Sir Arthur Conan Doyle, *The Complete Sherlock Holmes* (New York: Barnes and Noble, 2009), 15.

2. Ibid., 740–741.

3. A. W. Tozer, *The Knowledge of the Holy: The Attributes of God: Their Meaning in the Christian Life* (New York: HarperCollins, 1961), 1.

46. A Note on Music

1. Sir Arthur Conan Doyle, *The Complete Sherlock Holmes* (New York: Barnes and Noble, 2009), 7.

2. Ibid., 970.

3. Ibid., 856.

4. Jonathan Edwards, "188. Heaven," accessed November 25, 2014, https://tollelege.wordpress.com/2009/10/23/heaven-is-a-world-of-singing-by-jonathan-edwards/

47. Work It Out

1. Sir Arthur Conan Doyle, *The Complete Sherlock Holmes* (New York: Barnes and Noble, 2009), 361.

2. Ibid., 76.

3. Ibid., 458.

4. http://www.brainyquote.com/quotes/quotes/t/tseliot132678.html.

48. The Greatest Game

1. Sir Arthur Conan Doyle, *The Complete Sherlock Holmes* (New York: Barnes and Noble, 2009), 602.

2. http://shakespeare.mit.edu/henryv/henryv.3.1.html

3. 3. Sir Arthur Conan Doyle, The Complete Sherlock Holmes (New York: Barnes and Noble, 2009), 602.

49. INSIDE EVIL

    1. Sir Arthur Conan Doyle, *The Complete Sherlock Holmes* (New York: Barnes and Noble, 2009), 449.

    2. Ibid., 664.

    3. Thomas Watson, *Doctrine of Repentance* (Scotland:/ Banner of Truth, January 1, 1988), 63.

    4. Augustus Toplady, "Rock of Ages," accessed November 26, 2014, http://www.cyberhymnal.org/htm/r/o/rockages.htm.

50. HOLMES STUDY

    1. http://www.bakerstreetirregulars.com/.

51. THE IRON FIST

    1. Sir Arthur Conan Doyle, *The Complete Sherlock Holmes* (New York: Barnes and Noble, 2009), 82.

    2. Ibid.

    3. Ibid.

    4. Ibid.

52. FED UP

    1. Sir Arthur Conan Doyle, *The Complete Sherlock Holmes* (New York: Barnes and Noble, 2009), 475.

    2. Oswald Chambers, *My Utmost for His Highest* (Grand Rapids: Discovery House Publishers, 1963).

53. STATING THE OBVIOUS
1. Sir Arthur Conan Doyle, *The Complete Sherlock Holmes* (New York: Barnes and Noble, 2009), 160.

2. Ibid.

54. DOWNWARD BOUND
1. Sir Arthur Conan Doyle, *The Complete Sherlock Holmes* (New York: Barnes and Noble, 2009), 862.

55. CHARACTER MATTERS
1. Sir Arthur Conan Doyle, *The Complete Sherlock Holmes* (New York: Barnes and Noble, 2009), 273.

56. CONFESSION
1. Sir Arthur Conan Doyle, *The Complete Sherlock Holmes* (New York: Barnes and Noble, 2009), 5.

2. Ibid., 7.

3. Dietrich Bonhoeffer, *Life Together: The Classic Exploration of Faith in Community* (New York: HarperOne, 2009), chapter 5.

57. A MYSTERIOUS SOCIETY
1. http://www.bakerstreetirregulars.com/.

59. PERSON OF INTEREST
1. Sir Arthur Conan Doyle, *The Complete Sherlock Holmes* (New York: Barnes and Noble, 2009), 440.

2. Martin Luther, "A Mighty Fortress Is Our God," accessed November 26, 2014, http://www. cyberhymnal.org/htm/m/i/mightyfo.htm.

60. In the End

1. Sir Arthur Conan Doyle, *The Complete Sherlock Holmes* (New York: Barnes and Noble, 2009), 296.

2. Ibid., 310.

3. Ibid., 300.

4. Ibid., 1077.

Trisha White Priebe is a wife, mom, writer, editor, and shameless water polo enthusiast. She serves as an assistant to Jerry B. Jenkins, speaks at retreats, and enjoys assisting her husband in youth ministry. In 2011, she published my first book: *Trust, Hope, Pray: Encouragement for the Task of Waiting.*